Doležel, Lubomír.
Narrative modes in
Czech literature.

DISCARD

NARRATIVE MODES IN CZECH LITERATURE

LUBOMÍR DOLEŽEL

Narrative Modes
in Czech Literature

UNIVERSITY OF TORONTO PRESS

© University of Toronto Press 1973
Printed in Canada by
University of Toronto Press
Toronto and Buffalo
ISBN 0-8020-5276-2
LC 74-190343

Preface

This collection of essays is offered as a tribute to Czech literature and to the Prague school of structural linguistics and literary theory. In it an attempt is made to integrate the results of a structural analysis of some major works of Czech fiction into the general framework of a structurally-oriented literary theory. The essays, therefore, are presented so that they may be read without any knowledge of the Czech language or Czech literary history. All Czech examples and materials are translated into English, preserving traits of the original texts which are relevant for structural analysis. (For this reason, the existing English translations were used only after substantial revision.) The number assigned to each translated example in the text refers to the original Czech passage which is given in the Appendix.

All the essays are aimed primarily at one central problem in the theory of fiction: the problem of narrator. A brief outline of a structural classification of various types of narrator (*narrative modes*) is given in the Introduction. A documentation of the particular modes is then provided in the individual essays. The first essay attacks the problem of represented discourse; at the same time, however, it contributes to a better understanding of the general model proposed in the Introduction. The rest of the essays, while concentrating on the study of specific aspects of the narrator, bring some other components of the narrative structure, closely related to that of the narrator, into sharp focus. Thus, the investigation of Komenský's *Labyrinth* leads to a general scheme of the work's symmetrical composition. In the third essay, the role of the objective narrator in the over-all structure of a 'realistic' work is outlined. In the essay on Čapek and

Vančura, a contrastive typology of the 'traditional' and 'modern' narrative structure is suggested. Finally, in the last essay, the organization of narrative time in a modern fictional work is investigated in some detail.

All of the essays appear here for the first time in English. Only one of them, the study of Komenský's *Labyrinth*, was previously published in Czech (in *Česká literatura*, 1969). Although the investigation of represented discourse in Czech fiction is based on material which has been used in my previous publications, the texts published here differ substantially from my works published in Czech.

The essays of this collection grew out of my courses and lectures at The University of Michigan (1965–68) and at the University of Toronto (1969–70). My special thanks go to Professor John Mersereau Jr. and Professor Cathryn Feuer, heads of the two Slavic departments who were instrumental in introducing the study of Czech language and literature to their respective universities. Financial assistance for the research and the technical help was provided by the Center for Russian and East European Studies at The University of Michigan, by the Canada Council and by the Humanities and Social Sciences Committee at the University of Toronto.

Professor Irwin Titunik of The University of Michigan has made an extraordinary contribution to this collection; without his editorial help – based on a perfect understanding of my material and methodology – I would not have attempted to present these texts to the English reader. I am also indebted to Professor Thomas Winner, Professor Samuel R. Levin, and Mr Richard Weiss, MA, for their valuable comments, and to the staff of University of Toronto Press, especially Dr R. M. Schoeffel. Last but not least, I would like to acknowledge grants from the Humanities Research Council of Canada, using funds provided by the Canada Council, and from the University of Toronto Press Publications Fund that made publication of this book possible.

LD
Lion's Head, Ontario
1971

Contents

Abbreviations

s–text	speaker-oriented text
R–text	referent-oriented text
DC	characters' discourse
DN	narrator's discourse
DD	direct discourse
UDD	unmarked direct discourse
RD	represented discourse
N–motif	narrator's action-motif

NARRATIVE MODES IN CZECH LITERATURE

Introduction

Every narrative text is a plurality of discourses whose mutual relationships, contrasts and harmonies constitute the basis of verbal structure of the narrative genre. The pluralistic concept of narrative text was outlined in ancient poetics by Plato. Diomedes (in the fourth century AD) singled out this property as the main distinguishing feature of the narrative genre: the narrative genre (epopee) is *genus commune*, combining two differentiated discourses – the poet's speech (*modus enarativum*) and the characters' speech (*modus imitativum*). On the contrary, lyric and drama are 'simple' genres, lyric characterized by *modus enarativum* only and drama by *modus imitativum*.[1]

In modern times, much more complex and detailed schemes of the plurality of narrative discourses have been developed. The works of Russian scholars in the early 1930s[2] provide us with a comprehensive outline of the variety of narrative discourses, as well as of the variability of their relationships within a narrative text. Narrative text revealed its 'polyphonic' character; it appeared as a field of confrontation of numerous 'voices' which engage in polemics, attempt to dominate one another, produce echoes or join in harmony to pass on the narrative message. In the contemporary poetics of narrative texts, the pluralistic concept is quite apparent in the works of

1 Cf. E.R. Curtius, *Europäische Literatur und lateinisches Mittelalter*, Bern, 1948, p. 439f.

2 See esp.: M.M. Bachtin, *Problemy tvorčestva Dostojevskogo* [Problems of Dostoyevsky's Art], Moscow, 1929; V.N. Vološinov, *Marksizm i filosofija jazyka* [Marxism and the Philosophy of Language], Leningrad, 1930; V.V. Vinogradov, *O chudožestvennoj proze* [On Artistic Prose], Moscow – Leningrad, 1930.

French Structuralists, especially in Barthes's theory of the narrative text as a manifestation of a set of different 'codes',[3] or in the notion of *intertextualité* coined by Julia Kristeva.[4] Thus, modern trends in the poetics of narrative text have revealed the invalidity of a normative poetics which required that the narrative text possess a unity and harmony of style or tone or 'mode'; the literary practice of modern fiction had never, in any case, followed that prescription.

The variability of narrative discourses has many sources and many forms; therefore, it cannot be accounted for by a single model. It seems to me, however, that the fundamental forms of narrative discourses can be described on the axis:

narrator's discourse (DN) – characters' discourse (DC)

corresponding to the classic dichotomy proposed by Diomedes. Every narrative text T is a concatenation and alternation of DN and DC:

$$T \rightarrow DN + DC.$$

DN is commonly associated with the narrating medium (*narrator*), DC with the narrated characters (*dramatis personae*).

This simple model can be said to describe the 'deep' structure of narrative as genre (text type). However, the history of the genre amply shows that in the 'surface' structure, the dichotomy of DN and DC is much more complicated, due, primarily, to two circumstances:

1 Both DN and DC can be found to be expressed in a variety of forms; let us call the forms of DN *narrative modes* (n_1, n_2, ... , n_k), the forms of DC *modes of characters' speech* (c_1, c_2, ... , c_l). Scheme 1 gives a general representation of the narrative text structure on both the 'deep' and the 'surface' levels.

2 DN and DC are not separated and isolated discourses, but are characterized by a dynamic correlation, ranging from absolute dichotomy to complete assimilation. Various modes of N and C can be arranged on a continuous scale, where the 'basic' modes ($n_1 - c_l$) represent the extreme poles.

In this Introduction, a structural approach to the description of this scale will be suggested. In accordance with the general purpose of this book, we will focus on the typology of narrative modes; modes of characters' speech will be taken into account only insofar as necessary for our main purpose.

3 R. Barthes, S/Z, Paris, 1970.
4 J. Kristeva, *Le texte du roman*, The Hague – Paris, 1970.

Scheme 1

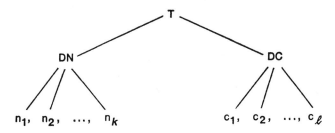

Criticism of fiction has devoted much attention to the study of the narrator and of various narrative modes.[5] In traditional criticism, this component of the narrative structure was treated primarily within the framework of the mimetic theory of fiction. Anthropomorphic concepts and personifying terms (such as: 'omniscient' narrator, narrator with 'limited omniscience') are characteristic of this approach. The textual base of the narrator was more or less overlooked.[6]

In this sketch of a structural typology of narrative modes, I do not want to do away completely with the traditional anthropomorphic terminology. (Even the term 'narrator' is of this nature!) At the same time, however, I would like to emphasize two essential assumptions on which the structural theory of narrator is based:

1 In the process of reading a narrative text, referential totalities (such as 'narrator', 'characters', etc.) are generated for the reader through the process of semantic accumulation. However, these referential totalities are secondary with respect to their textual base. Nothing is in the referent that had not been expressed – explicitly or implicitly – in the text. It can be

5 In 1910 the first monograph devoted to the problem was published in Germany: K. Friedemann's *Die Rolle des Erzählers in der Epik*, Leipzig, 1910. A sample of more recent works: N. Friedman, 'Point of View in Fiction', *PMLA*, LXX (1955); W. Kayser, 'Wer erzählt den Roman?' in *Vortragsreise. Studien zur Literatur*, Bern, 1958; Wayne C. Booth, *The Rhetoric of Fiction*, Chicago – London, 1961; I. Titunik, 'The Problem of "Skaz" in Russian Literature', PhD. Dissertation, University of California, Berkeley, 1963; K.F. Stanzel, *Typische Formen des Romans*, Göttingen, 1964; L. Doležel, 'The Typology of the Narrator: Point of View in Fiction' in *To Honor Roman Jakobson*, The Hague – Paris, 1967, vol. I; F. van Rossum-Guyon, 'Point de vue ou perspective narrative', *Poétique*, IV (1970).

6 Cf. the following explicit statement: 'Ce qui relève de la technique proprement romanesque est au fond, pour les significations mêmes du roman, accessoire et nous ne nous y attacherons guère ... Ce qui nous intéresse, c'est l'anthropologie qu'il (le roman), selon les cas, révèle ou suggère ou enfin suscite dans l'esprit du lecteur.' (J. Pouillon, *Temps et roman*, Paris, 1946, p. 36.)

claimed that the shortcomings and inconsistencies of the extant typologies of narrator are due primarily to neglect of the textual base.

2 Referential totalities – as components of the overall text referent – are semiotic in nature; the referent (or any of its components) is a dimension of the text sign. The epistemological nature of narrator, character, etc., is fundamentally different from that of 'real' people.

In order to arrive at a structural typology of narrator, two aspects of narrator will be taken into account: *functional* and *verbal*. It follows from the basic dichotomy of the narrative structure that the functions and verbal features of the narrator can be specified only in opposition to those of characters.

1 The functional model

Let us consider first a set of functions which are necessary to generate the 'deep' structure of the narrative text (DN + DC); the functions of this set will be called *obligatory* or *primary* functions.

a) With respect to the narrated events, the narrator fulfills the function of *representation*. The narrator is the verbal medium of narrated events. The first obligatory function of characters is their participation in the narrated events; the *dramatis personae* are prime movers, active agents of the narrated actions. Let us call this participation in the narrated events the *action* function. It need hardly be said that the action function is not obligatory with the narrator.

b) The representational function of the narrator is always coupled with the *controlling* function: the narrator dominates the narrative text structure. The controlling function of the narrator manifests itself in the incorporation of DC into the framework of DN; by no means does it imply any kind of control of the characters' 'behaviour'. Explicit devices of the controlling function are expressed in DN: introductory phrases, specification of the intonation, tone of the characters' speeches, etc. No such reference to DN can be found in DC.

The second obligatory function of characters will be called *interpretative*. I have in mind the fact that each character expresses in his discourse a set of idiosyncratic (subjective) attitudes toward the narrated events. Through the interpretative function, discourses of particular characters are differentiated in their 'subjective semantics'; explicit commentaries, evaluations and reactions are the most conspicuous devices of the interpretative function.

Let us now turn to the optional, secondary functions of the narrator and characters, which will be used to explain the 'surface' structure of the narrative text. It should be noted that secondary functions result from a functional shift: the narrator may take up, as his secondary functions, the primary functions of characters; or the primary functions of narrator may be taken up by characters, becoming their secondary functions.

c) The narrator can take up the function of *interpretation* by expressing specific attitudes, comments and evaluations regarding the narrated events. Through the effect of the interpretative function, the character of DN changes dramatically.

d) The narrator can take up the *action* function by becoming an active agent of the narrated actions. Simply speaking, the narrator can be identical with one of the *dramatis personae* of the action. This shift is, of course, identical with the character's taking over the *representational* function. Because of the coupling of the narrator's functions a) and b), the character assumes in this case also the controlling function. We arrive here at a full assimilation of the narrator with (a) character: one and the same component of the narrative structure is assigned both sets of primary functions – those of the narrator, and those of the characters. The opposition of narrator and character is 'neutralized'.

Let us now summarize, in Scheme 2, the sets of primary and secondary functions outlined above. By introducing the oriented arrow into the scheme, I mean to indicate the dynamic character of the relationship between the particular functions; the sign '&' symbolizes the coupling of functions:

Scheme 2

	Narrator	Character
1 Primary Functions	a) representation & b) control ↓	action ↑ interpretation ↑
2 Secondary Functions	c) interpretation ↓ d) action ⟶	control & representation

On the basis of this functional model, we can take the first step towards a structural typology of narrative modes; it is represented in Table 1.

By introducing the well-known formal distinction between the *Er*-form (third-person narrative) and *Ich*-form (first-person narrative),[7] the second

---

[7] Second-person narrative, used as an experiment by some contemporary writers, is not accounted for by our model; it requires a special study.

Table 1

Function \ Narrative Mode	representation	interpretation	action
objective	+	−	−
rhetorical	+	+	−
subjective	+	+	+

step of the classification procedure is made; the result of the two steps is the typology of narrative modes suggested in Scheme 3. I have tried to select as simple terminology as possible for the particular modes; for the sake of continuity, traditional terms have been preserved, wherever they did not seem misleading. I am convinced, however, that a less descriptive terminology would be – in the final outcome – more suitable for the structural theory (for example, the objective narrator could be called 'zero' narrator, etc.).

Scheme 3

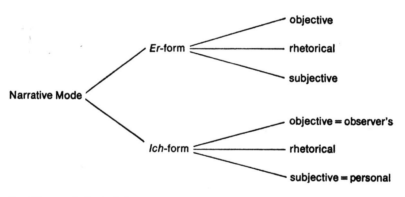

2 The verbal model

It has been indicated that the base for the typology of narrative modes is to be sought in the verbal structure of DN. Now, we can point to the shifts in the system of narrator's functions as to the source of the shifts in the verbal structure of DN. Therefore, the typology resulting from the verbal model should be identical to that suggested in Scheme 3; however, the dynamic character of the transition from one narrative mode to another should become more apparent in the verbal model.

We assume that the 'deep' structure of the narrative text – expressed in the dichotomy of DN and DC – can be represented by a set of binary text features. Elsewhere in this book (pp. 16, 20–40), a specification of these features is given. Here, I would like only to outline the relationship between the binary verbal model and the typology of narrative modes (which emerge on the 'surface' level of the narrative text structure). This relationship is represented in Table 2; in it, 0 symbolizes the negative value of the feature, 1 its positive value, 1/0 positive or negative; index ^{a} indicates that the feature refers to a narrator involved in the action (a narrator with action function).

It is apparent that this typology, although based on the verbal model, must take into account the functional model – by distinguishing feature 1 from feature 1^a. The 'cooperation' of the two models becomes even more necessary if we try to set up a structural typology of all modes of narrative discourse appearing on the axis DN ↔ DC. Scheme 4 offers a representation of this typology; it can be said to specify the narrative modes and modes of characters' speech, introduced in abstract terms in Scheme 1.

Circular representation has been used to suggest the continuity of the transition from pole n_1 – specified as objective *Er*-form – to pole c_i – specified as direct discourse. We can say that the 'deep' structure dichotomy of DN and DC is represented – on the 'surface' level – by the opposition of objective *Er*-form and direct discourse; the other modes are formed by the 'neutralization' of this opposition.

Several critical points in Scheme 4 require special comment:

1 The distinction between direct discourse and the personal *Ich*-form is purely functional; in their verbal structure, both modes of narrative discourse are identical. In other words, the personal *Ich*-form is the direct discourse of a character carrying out representational function.

2 Similarly, the distinction between the personal and the rhetorical *Ich*-forms must be made – as already indicated – on functional grounds. The verbal structure of the two modes is identical. The functional distinction (which in Table 2 was indicated by index ^{a}) is given by the presence (in the personal form) or the absence (in the rhetorical form) of the action function with the narrator.

3 The distinction between represented discourse and the subjective *Er*-form is, on the contrary, defined solely by the verbal model. Only a consistent or inconsistent occurrence of pertinent positive text features gives us a criterion for deciding whether we have to characterize a discourse as represented 'reproduction' of a character's speech or as a portion of subjective *Er*-narrative. Since this distinction is crucial from the point of view of both the theory and its application in concrete text analyses, a detailed discussion of the problem is presented in this book (pp. 50–55).

Table 2

Text Features / Narrative Mode	system of persons	system of tenses	deixis	allocution	emotive function	subjective semantics	specified speech level
personal *Ich*-form	1ə	1ə	1ə	1ə	1ə	1ə	1ə
subjective *Er*-form	0	0	1ə/0	1ə/0	1ə/0	1ə/0	1ə/0
objective *Er*-form	0	0	0	0	0	0	0
rhetorical *Er*-form	0	0	1	1	1	1	1
observer's *Ich*-form	1	1	0	0	0	0	0
rhetorical *Ich*-form	1	1	1	1	1	1	1

Scheme 4

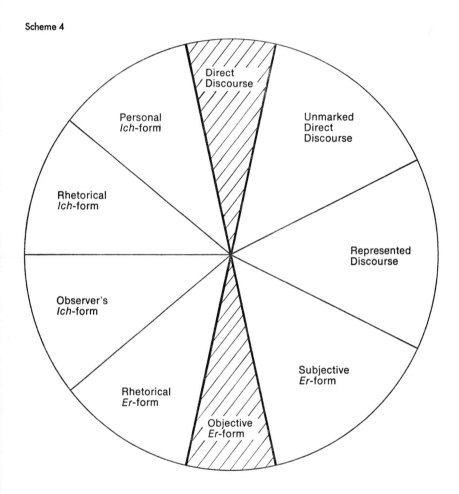

The points raised in 1, 2 and 3 above clearly show the complementary character of the functional and the verbal models. Some modes, which are ambiguous in terms of one model, can be distinguished by reference to the second model. But, it should be emphasized that no theoretical 'solution' will eliminate ambiguity from narrative texts. Discourse ambiguity seems to be an inherent property of the narrative text structure, resulting from the dynamic character of the opposition DN – DC. The very existence of this opposition – which, as we know, is essential for the narrative genre – creates immanent formal and semantic tensions within the text; in some narrative texts, these tensions are resolved by a rigid separation of DN and DC, in others, by their assimilation ('neutralization'), inevitably leading to discourse ambiguity.

The typology of narrative modes is the base for the structural theory of narrator. However, narrative modes are rather broad categories with a considerable flexibility and rich 'internal' variability. Two main sources of the variability can be pointed out. First, a narrative mode can be modelled on various extra-literary discourses. Thus, for example, the *Ich*-form modes can adopt features of memoirs, a diary, chronicle, exchange of letters (epistolary novel), oral story-telling, interior speech (stream-of consciousness technique), etc. Second, a narrative mode will be moulded in accordance with the general principles of a writer's idiosyncratic style. Idiosyncratic stylization opens the possibility of infinite variation within one and the same narrative mode. Every writer is given the opportunity to experiment in an original way with the given narrative modes. The study of narrative styles is fascinating on its own merits; however, it will gain a firm theoretical base only when the idiosyncratic styles are related to the underlying systems of narrative modes.

The particular narrative modes, defined by functions and verbal features, provide, as already indicated, the explanation of the semiotic 'effects' which have been traditionally identified with the narrator (with the 'image' of the narrator). The gamut of 'images' follows the gamut of narrative modes, ranging from the 'impartial' and 'anonymous' narrator of the objective *Er*-form to the narrator with the 'limited point-of-view' to the fully personalized narrator of the personal *Ich*-form.

The 'image' of the narrator can be directly related to the narrative mode as its referent. On the other hand, the relationship between the narrator and the author – so often treated in criticism of fiction – is indirect and 'exterior'. The history of fiction amply shows that there is no pre-determined connection between the author of a narrative text and its narrator.[8]

8 The relationship between the author and the narrator in narrative prose is analogous

This distinction is now an axiom of serious literary criticism.[9] On the other hand, the strict theoretical distinction of narrator and author does not preclude discovering affinities (ideological, biographical, etc.) between the author and his narrator (cf. here, p. 64); these affinities can assume a substantial importance for the structural interpretation of a narrative work.

The structural and semiotic theory of the narrative genre has made impressive advances in the last decades. The narrative structure has been investigated on various levels and in its various components. Since the narrator represents one of the central components of narrative structure, the theory of narrator assumes a crucial importance within the general theory of the narrative genre. The structural and semiotic approach enables us to penetrate from the rich variability and seeming uniqueness of narrators to the underlying narrative systems. It is hoped that illuminating insights into the structure and history of the narrative genre will be gained by a confrontation of the general models of narrative systems (proposed in this Introduction) with the variability of concrete manifestations investigated in the following essays of this collection.

to the relationship between the poet and the lyrical subject (the lyrical 'I') in lyric poetry. The variability of this relationship was pointed out by V. Erlich: 'It changes from work to work, from poet to poet, and from style to style. The lyrical "I" can be, for all practical purposes, a fictitious character. By the same token, he can express or impersonate the poet with an almost embarrassing directness, or at least purport to do so.' ('The Concept of the Poet as a Problem of Poetics' in *Poetics-Poetyka-Poetika*, Warsaw – The Hague, 1961, p. 709.)

9 Thus, for W. Kayser (p. 91) it is beyond doubt that 'der Erzähler in aller Erzählkunst niemals der bekannte oder noch unbekannte Autor ist, sondern eine Rolle, die der Autor erfindet und einnimmt'. R. Barthes requires a strict distinction to be made between 'l'auteur (matériel) d'un récit' and 'le narrateur de ce récit'. 'Les signes du narrateur sont immanents au récit.' ('Introduction à l'analyse structurale des récits', *Communications*, VIII (1966), p. 19.)

WORKS QUOTED IN CHAPTER I

ČF   K. Čapek, *The First Rescue Party*
ČH   K. Čapek, *Hordubal*
ČK   K. Čapek, *Krakatit*
OC   J. Otčenášek, *Citizen Brych*
ON   I. Olbracht, *Nikola Šuhaj, Robber*
PF   M. Pujmanová, *Playing with Fire*
PL   M. Pujmanová, *Life Against Death*
PP   M. Pujmanová, *People on the Crossroads*
PPr   M. Pujmanová, *Premonition*
VF   E. Valenta, *Follow the Green Light*

1
Represented discourse in modern Czech narrative prose

One of the most important tasks in the structural study of narrative prose is a thorough investigation of the relationship between the narrator's discourse (DN) and the characters' discourse (DC). The opposition of the two discourses can be said to represent the 'deep' level of the verbal structure in every narrative text. DN consists of segments of monologic discourse, the source of which is identifiable with the narrator. DC is an aggregate of both monologic and dialogic discourses which can be assigned to the particular acting characters of the story.

In order to describe the opposition of DN and DC and its inherent dynamism, let us introduce a text model based on Bühler's well-known 'triangle' of text functions.[1] Bühler's model assumes that text T is characterized by three function-relations: the *expressive* function – the relationship to speaker S; the *allocutional* function – the relationship to hearer H; and the *referential* function – the relationship to referent R (subject of text).[2] Let us now consider text model T' which is characterized by the relationship to the referent only (by the referential function only), lacking the relationship to both speaker and hearer. Schematically, the two models can be represented as follows:

1 K. Bühler, *Sprachtheorie*, Jena, 1934.
2 Cf. R. Jakobson, 'Linguistics and Poetics' in T. A. Sebeok (ed.), *Style in Language*, New York, 1960, esp. p. 355, and E. Benveniste, 'De la subjectivité dans le langage', *Journal de psychologie* (Jul.-Sept. 1958); (reprinted in *Problèmes de linguistique général*, Paris, 1966).

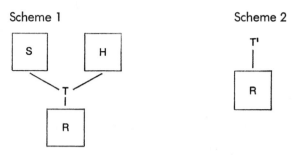

In Scheme 1, the speaker's control of the text structure is quite explicit; the model will therefore be called the *speaker-oriented text* (s-text). In Scheme 2, the controlling function of the speaker is void and its verbal structure is determined by the referent only; for this reason, the model will be called the *referent-oriented text* (r-text). Figuratively speaking, we can say that s-text provides some information about the speaker (and, potentially, also about the hearer) in addition to information about the referent; in r-text, the first kind of information is not expressed and only information about the referent is given.

The presence or absence of the speaker's explicit control is the determinant of the opposition of s-text and r-text. Under the speaker's control, certain verbal means of the text acquire additional qualities which are absent when the speaker's control is void. These qualities – I suggest calling them *discriminative text features* – are obviously of a binary nature; they assume a positive value in s-text and a negative ('zero') value in r-text.

A detailed description of discriminative features will be given in the first part of this essay. Here let us give just one illustrative example: Certain grammatical means, for example the persons of the verb, acquire the quality of *shifters* in s-text.[3] The use of persons follows the shifts in the functions of speaker, hearer and referent which, of course, can be assigned alternately to the participants of a speech act. In r-text, however, the persons of the verb cannot be used as shifters because of the lack of 'shifting reference'; in this case, we will say that the persons of the verb are used *absolutely*. In terms of our model, the quality of verbal person being used as shifter represents the positive value of the discriminative text feature; its quality of being used absolutely represents the negative value of the feature. Let us emphasize once more that linguistic means acquire the quality of discriminative features (positive or negative) within the framework of a text only; outside this framework the quality is not describable.

3 The notion of shifters was introduced by R. Jakobson in *Shifters, Verbal Categories and the Russian Verb*, Cambridge, Mass., 1957.

Let us now return from the level of our abstract model to the empirical level of DN and DC in the verbal structure of narrative prose. We will begin our analysis of this opposition by introducing the notion of *traditional narrative text*. A narrative text will be called 'traditional' (T_t) if DN is equivalent to R-text and DC to s-text; symbolically:

$$T_t \rightarrow (DN \equiv R) + (DC \equiv S).$$

In other words, in the traditional text, DN will reveal no traces of the speaker and his organizing control, while in DC the speaker and his control will be felt without any restrictions. The narrator's discourse of the traditional text is based on a total repression of any reference to the speaker; in the characters' discourse, reference to the speaker, shifting in accordance with the alternations of speaking characters, manifests itself explicitly and to the same extent as, for example, in oral conversation. Traditionally, this form of DC is called 'direct discourse' (DD). All these statements are true only of third-person narrative (*Er*-form); in first-person narrative (*Ich*-form), we face a special situation, since a character (more or less involved in the story) assumes the representational function. The implications of this special situation for our investigation will be discussed later (pp. 23–6).

The clear-cut opposition of DN and DC implies that in the *sequential structure* of the traditional narrative text, alternating segments of DN and DC are precisely and unambiguously demarcated from one another. Usually, this demarcation is emphasized by the use of conventional punctuation marks. Thus, a narrative text of the traditional type is *a sequence of maximally differentiated and precisely demarcated segments of DN and DC*.

It has to be noted in this connection that literary texts can be described on two levels: on the level of abstract type, and on that of concrete manifestations (particular works). The structure of type can be expressed in terms of *norms* which are assumed to be reflected in the particular manifestations. However, because of the flexible character of literary norms, structures of particular manifestations cannot be expected to reflect the type structure perfectly. Occasional violations of, or deviations from, the norm(s) cannot affect our attribution of a certain concrete narrative text to a specific text type (cf. here, pp. 65, 96).[4]

---

4 For a discussion of the term 'literary (aesthetic) norm', see J. Mukařovský, *Estetická funkce, norma a hodnota* [Aesthetic Function, Norm and Value], Prague, 1936 (reprinted in *Studie z estetiky*, Prague, 1966; English translation published in *Michigan Slavic Contributions*, Ann Arbor, Mich., 1970 vol. III). The relationship between literary type and literary work was outlined by K.F. Stanzel in *Typische Formen des Romans*, Göttingen, 1964.

In this sense, the history of narrative prose offers numerous manifestations of the traditional narrative text, especially in nineteenth-century realistic fiction. Let us quote here, for the sake of illustration, a randomly selected portion of the novel *The Grandmother* (*Babička*) by the popular Czech realist Božena Němcová (1820–62); this portion exemplifies not only the R-text character of narrative, but also the use of verbal and pronominal shifters in the speech of characters, resulting from the alternation of two speakers – participants in the dialogue (symbolized as A and B):

1/ A: 'I came to see how you are enjoying yourself today, John,' the princess addressed her groom.

B: 'Your Highness, it is always very pleasant with my family and a few good friends,' Mr. Prošek answered.

A: 'Who is with you?'

B: 'My neighbours, the miller and his family and the forester from Ryznburg.'

A: 'Don't let me disturb you. Go back to them. I'll leave you.' Mr. Prošek bowed, not daring to detain his master.

Discriminative text features coupled with punctuation marks make possible a clear and unequivocal segmentation of Němcová's text; its sequential structure can be easily established as follows:

$$\text{DC}(\text{A}) \ // \ \text{DN} \ // \ \text{DC}(\text{B}) \ // \ \text{DN} \ // \ \text{DC}(\text{A}) \ / \ \text{DC}(\text{B}) \ / \ \text{DC}(\text{A}) \ // \ \text{DN}$$

With the development of modern fiction, the relationship between DN and DC underwent a dramatic change. In structural terms, this change can be described as a process of "neutralization', i.e. a process of abolishing the opposition of the two planes.[5] As a result, a transitional zone has come into prominence, represented in the sequential structure of narrative texts by the occurrence of more or less frequent ambiguous segments. The most important device of this ambiguity is the so-called *represented discourse* (hereafter RD).

RD can be called a truly 'international', universal narrative device. It has been described practically in all occidental literatures.[6] There is no doubt

---

5 In a wider framework, I have dealt with this process in several publications, especially: *O stylu moderní české prózy* [On the Style of Modern Czech Prose], Prague, 1960; 'Nejtralizacija protivopostavlenij v jazykovo-stilističeskoj strukture epičeskoj prozy' [Neutralization of Oppositions in the Stylistic Structure of Narrative Prose] in *Problemy sovremennoj filologii*, Moscow, 1965, pp. 116–23; 'The Typology of the Narrator' in *To Honor Roman Jakobson*, The Hague, 1967, vol. I, pp. 541–52.

6 Recently RD was described in modern Chinese fiction; see J. Průšek, 'Quelques re-

that the very existence of such a universal device clearly demonstrates that the idea of 'world literature' is highly meaningful with respect to literary forms and structures. Apparently, there exists a 'stock' of literary devices which can be used and modified in any national literature and by any individual writer, regardless of his philosophical or ideological position.

Because of the rich implementation of RD in the modern prose of many nations, investigation of RD has been a central concern of a great number of linguists and literary scholars. Moreover, soon after its 'discovery', RD became for quite some time 'the apple of discord' between German and French (i.e., Geneva school) scholars. Their discussions and polemics are still rather instructive because they reflect two quite different ways of analyzing and interpreting literary devices.

For German scholars, mostly of the Vossler school, RD was a phenomenon of the *Sprachseele*. Wrapping their ideas in rather vague terminology, they were, nevertheless, able to sketch a plausible theory of RD: RD was treated in the general framework of the relationship between narrator and characters in fiction; it emerged as a 'mixed', transitional device. Thus, for example, for E. Lorck, RD is character utterance 'experienced' (*erlebt*) by the narrator. According to E. Lerch, in RD the speech of the character is transmitted not as 'reported' speech, but as 'reality' stated by the narrator.[7] Speculating in such pseudo-psycholinguistic terms, the German scholars paid no attention to the formal, linguistic features of RD.

On the other side, for Ch. Bally and his disciples (primarily M. Lips), RD was a device of 'reporting', of reproducing another's speech. RD expanded the traditional repertoire of reporting devices – direct and indirect discourse; the distinction between RD and the traditional devices had to do with verbal form only, RD being, in Bally's opinion, a transform of indirect discourse.[8] Even in his last work on this problem, Bally, polemicizing with Lerch and Spitzer, persists in maintaining that RD is 'a grammatical device of pure reproduction'.[9] In accordance with their theory, scholars of Bally's school concentrated on verbal, especially grammatical, features of RD.

Later investigations of RD vacillated between the German 'psycholog-

marques sur la nouvelle littérature chinoise' in *Mélanges de Sinologie offerts à M. Paul Demiéville*, Paris, 1966, esp. p. 218.

7 E. Lorck, *Die 'erlebte Rede'*, Heidelberg, 1921; E. Lerch, 'Ursprung und Bedeutung der sog. "erlebten Rede" (Rede als Tatsache)', Germanisch-Romanische Monatsschrift (hereafter cited as *GRM*), xvi (1928), pp. 459–78.

8 Ch. Bally, 'Le style indirect libre en français moderne', *GRM* iv (1912), pp. 549–56, 597–606; M. Lips, *Style indirect libre*, Paris, 1926.

9 Ch. Bally, 'Antiphrase et style indirect libre' in *A Grammatical Miscellany Offered to Otto Jespersen*, Copenhagen – London, 1930, p. 331.

ical' theory and Bally's 'grammatical' theory. Thus, for example, in Russian scholarship, V.N. Vološinov came closer to the German concept, whereas I.I. Koftunova and N.S. Pospelov, concentrating on the verbal features of RD, naturally inclined toward Bally's position.[10] In Czech, RD has been analyzed almost exclusively from a purely linguistic point of view, in the general framework of syntactical description of various forms of 'reported speech'.[11]

Taken in this historical context, our approach can be epitomized as a certain kind of synthesis: We will consider RD a transitional narrative device, resulting from the neutralization of the opposition of DN and DC. At the same time, however, the verbal, linguistic character of the device will be emphasized. It is hoped that we shall succeed in demonstrating the specific merits of the structural approach in the course of our analysis and in the results obtained.

I DISCRIMINATIVE FEATURES IN CZECH RD

It has already been indicated that the problem of RD in Czech will be treated in the wider theoretical framework of the 'neutralization' of the opposition of DN and DC. Whereas in their binary opposition (as manifested in the traditional narrative text), DN and DC are characterized by an accumulation of negative and positive discriminative features respectively, narrative devices arising from the process of 'neutralization' will combine in their verbal structure both positive and negative values of the discriminative features. In this sense, all these devices – above all RD – will be structurally 'mixed' and, therefore, latently ambiguous. The investigation of the particular discriminative text features which follows is aimed at establishing the combination of positive and negative values of the features typifying RD.

---

10 V.N. Vološinov, *Marksizm i filosofija jazyka* [Marxism and the Philosophy of Language], Leningrad, 1930; I.I. Koftunova, 'Nesobstvenno-prjamaja reč' v sovremennom russkom literaturnom jazyke' [Represented Discourse in Contemporary Standard Russian], *Russkij jazyk v škole*, no. 2 (1953), pp. 18–27; N.S. Pospelov, 'Nesobstvenno-prjamaja reč i formy jeje vyraženija v chudožestvennoj proze Gončarova 30–40-ch godov' [Represented Discourse and Forms of its Expression in the Artistic Prose of Gončarov in the 30s and 40s] in *Materialy i issledovanija po istorii russkogo literaturnogo jazyka*, Moscow, 1957, vol. IV, pp. 218–39.

11 J. Haller, 'Řeč přímá, nepřímá a polopřímá' [Direct, Indirect and Represented Discourse], *Naše řeč*, XIII (1929), pp. 97–107, 121–30; F. Trávníček, *Mluvnice spisovné češtiny* [Grammar of Standard Czech], 3rd. ed., Prague, 1951, vol. II, pp. 748–51.

1 System of grammatical persons in RD

The fundamental formal discriminative feature of DC and DN is the system and use of grammatical persons. (I am discussing specifically grammatical persons of the verb, but all statements refer also to personal pronouns.) DC is characterized by a three-person system, with the well-known scheme of functions: the first – relating the verbal action to the speaker; the second – relating it to the hearer; the third – assigning the action to the referent (to the object of utterance, the person or thing – the who or what – talked about). As already mentioned (p. 16), grammatical persons in DC behave as shifters, i.e. their usage is subject to shifts, determined by the shifts of the speaking agent.

In contrast, in DN, where the relations to both the speaker and the hearer are void, verbal action can be assigned only to the referent (object of utterance). This results in DN having only a one-form system of grammatical persons. The form is equivalent to the third-person formation.

If we now direct our attention to RD, we can rather easily confirm earlier findings of its essential differentiation from DC in the system of grammatical persons. Let us compare two simple dialogues between two characters, one in the 'pure' DC form of 'direct discourse' (DD), another in RD. For ease of understanding, I have separated the particular speeches into paragraphs and symbolized the participants as A and B:

2a/ A: 'Where is your workman?'
   B: 'At home, in Rybáry.'
   A: 'How do you know that?'
   B: 'Well – I only think –'
   A: 'I am not asking you what you think. How do you know that he's in Rybáry?'
   B: '– I don't.' [ČH]

2b/ A: Mister's a stranger here?
   B: Yes, that's right, a stranger. He's just moved in and doesn't know things here yet, and he's going to be living here permanently.
   A: Then, of course, ... he's going to need someone to do his laundry once in a while. Has he found a woman in Dolina to do his laundry for him?
   B: Oh ... he hadn't even given it a thought, and that's no small matter. [VF]

As can readily be seen, the two dialogues yield quite different effects because of the different use of grammatical persons. In the DD dialogue, constant alternations of persons occur, following the alternations of reference and the shifts of functions of the two participants in the speech act. On the other hand, the RD dialogue lacks the formal distinction of grammatical persons and, therefore, lacks that kind of alternation. Reduction of grammatical persons to one – formally equivalent with the third person – gives the dialogue a strange, muted quality.

A detailed analysis reveals the following use of grammatical persons in Czech RD:

a) The reference to the speaker is expressed by the third person, both in the singular, and in the plural (italics in the following examples are mine – LD):

3/ TORGLER: *He thanks* both gentlemen for their good will; but *he knows* that *his* case is in the best possible hands and *he is asking* Doctor Sack only to act for *him* as he sees fit. [PF]

4/ SOLDIERS: Maybe mister has a few pairs of shoes that he hadn't time to get polished up during this miserable weather. *They'd shine* them up for him so they'd gleam like a mirror. *They don't want* money for it, but *they'd appreciate* a piece of bread. [VF]

b) The reference to the hearer is also expressed by the third person. Singular is used for both 'thee' and 'you'; plural refers to an addressee consisting of more than one person:

5/ POLICEMAN: 'How are you, Eržika?' ... No, *she mustn't be* afraid, he hasn't come officially. [ON]

6/ SERGEANT: If *they bring* him Nikola *they'd get* money for drinks. If not, *they'll* immediately *be conscripted* and sent to the front. [ON]

c) The grammatical person of the referent (object of utterance) is, naturally, the third, both in singular, and in plural:

7/ STANDA: What *will* the party *think?* – *they* all *did* a hundred times more ... even that beast Matula, and Pepek with *his* jawing. [ČF]

Only in one special case do we find verbal forms in RD in other grammatical persons than the third. That occurs in sentences with an indefinite (general) subject. In my material, I have evidence primarily of the type using the second person singular (aside from the most common type using the subject *člověk* – corresponding to the English use of 'one' – which, with its third person, does not, of course, constitute an exception). Here is one example of the you-indefinite subject:

8/ RÁŽ: He knew her. She is sensitive, changeable as spring weather, violent one instant and dreamy and soft the next. And pig-headed! *You can't* get to her by direct attack, but if *you know* her, *you can* play the keyboard of her moods and frailties like a virtuoso. [OC]

Some other forms that have been found in RD, for example *řekněme* ('let us say'), *myslím* ('I think'), etc., do not operate as verbs, but rather as adverbs. Just the possibility of their being used in RD indicates how far the 'adverbialization' of these verbal forms has advanced. It is essential to note that all of these exceptional cases can also occur in DN. This shows that in these cases verbal persons are not treated as shifters as they are in the regular instances. In other words, these cases are not exceptions with respect to RD, but with respect to Czech grammar in general. Thus, a one-person system is confirmed to be an eminent verbal feature of RD in Czech. The same, apparently, holds about RD in other languages as well.

This statement, however, applies to third-person narrative only. As already indicated, first-person narrative (*Ich*-form) represents a quite different case; its analysis brings results which, in my opinion, are extremely important for the theory of RD. As far as I know, features of RD in *Ich*-form have not been investigated. The main reason, undoubtedly, is the rarity of this variant of RD. Only RD dialogues provide reliable material; RD interior monologues in *Ich*-form (only narrator's interior monologues can be expected) coalesce formally with the narrative and cannot be distinguished from it (unless clumsy introductory phrases, such as 'I thought to myself', are used). In contemporary Czech literature, we find frequent and original use of RD dialogues in Edvard Valenta's novel *Follow the Green Light* (*Jdi za zeleným světlem*, 1956); the chapters called 'Intermezzi' are narrated in the first person by the protagonist, Professor Šimon, alternating with chapters told in the third-person narrative.[12]

DN of the Ich-form is characterized by a two-person system: the first person, referring to the *Ich*-narrator, and the third person, relating the action to the referent (to the 'narrated events'). A detailed analysis of material confirmed our surmise that RD in *Ich*-form narrative would employ an equivalent system of grammatical persons. To describe the functions of persons in this variant of RD, we have to distinguish the *Ich*-narrator as

12 The shifts of *Er*- and *Ich*-form narrative in *Follow the Green Light* are described briefly here, p. 114.

participant in dialogues – we will call him N-speaker and N-hearer – from all other participants (other characters who participate in dialogues). The grammatical persons in RD are then assigned the following functions:

*a) The N-speaker is referred to in the first person singular; the reference to a group in which the N-speaker is a member is expressed by the first person plural:

9/ ŠIMON: Thanks, for the time being *I'm not starving.* As he sees, Mr. Pohořelý takes excellent care of *me.* [VF]

10/ ŠIMON: *We could* move downstairs later on to *my* place where *we won't* disturb anybody. [VF]

a) The reference to a speaker other than the narrator is expressed by the third person:

11/ TEREBA: *He assumed he had bought* goods complete. [VF]

12/ THE FORESTER: *They* always *play* on a Saturday or before a holiday when there's no need to get up the next morning. [VF]

*b) The person of the N-hearer is the first person singular; the difference between 'thee' and 'you' is not expressed:

13/ BLANKA addressing ŠIMON: If *I don't have* a spare moment for imagination ... *I ought* at least to tie some kind of ribbon around the envelope or have Blanka do it. [VF]

14/ TEREBA speaking to ŠIMON: So, if *I were* kind enough not to forget the purpose of *my* visit, he would first of all find out *my* collar size and the measurement of *my* waist and sleeves. [VF]

The use of plural in this function is a curious phenomenon. It is always used to express the reference to a group of which the N-hearer is a member. However, two different instances are covered by this form:

*b₁) A group of addressees including the narrator; here the first person plural in RD corresponds to the second person plural in DD (you = you + you):

15/ A POLICEMAN addressing ŠIMON and BLANKA: The only important thing right now is that *we be not* too severe when she returns. ... In any case, *we should phone* immediately when she comes home, so that they won't worry for no reason. [vf]

*b₂) A group consisting of the n-hearer and the speaker, different from the narrator; here the first person in RD corresponds to the first person plural in DD (we = I + you):

16/ ELIŠKA speaking to ŠIMON: *We would have* two-and-a-half hours for *ourselves*; she had figured that out from the timetable. [vf]

b) The reference to the hearer other than the narrator is expressed by the third person. Although I have only examples of the singular, we may assume that a group of hearers would be, correspondingly, referred to by the third person plural:

17/ ŠIMON addressing SLÁVKA: *Couldn't* Slávka *hit* a choice rabbit over the head? ... *Doesn't* Slávka *have* a basket for mushrooms that *she could part* with for a few days? [vf]

c) Finally, as might be expected, reference to the object of utterance (referent) is expressed by the third person, either singular or plural:

18/ TŘÍSKA: An army *rolls* straight on, road or no road; *they drive* their tanks right over the fields; *they make* their horses go right through the crops. [vf]

In summary, the results of our analysis of grammatical persons in RD can be expressed by a set of simple transformations, taking the three-person system of DC as the underlying structure. For RD of the third-person narrative, the following transformations apply (both in singular and in plural):

first person	→	third person
second person	→	third person
third person	→	third person

In the first-person narrative, the same set of transformations applies, but only in the cases a), b), c) (with the speaker and hearer different from the *Ich*-narrator); in cases *a) and *b) (including *b₁ and *b₂), concerning the n-speaker and the n-hearer (as an individual or as a member of a group), a different set of transformations applies:

| *first person | → | first person |
| *second person | → | first person |

If we compare the results of the transformations with the system of grammatical persons in DN (in the *Er*-form and *Ich*-form respectively), we can formulate a general transformational rule:

The system of grammatical persons of RD *is obtained when transforming the three-person system in such a way as to arrive at a system formally identical with that of* DN.

It is this general rule which, in my opinion, should be considered a basic statement of the theory of RD. It implies that with respect to the most conspicuous formal difference between DN and DC, RD is identical with DN by adopting a system of grammatical persons equivalent to that of DN: In the third-person narrative, DN is characterized by a one-person system (formally identical with the third person); correspondingly, RD here adopts a one-person (third-person) system. In the *Ich*-form, DD is characterized by a system of two persons (first and third); correspondingly, RD in this form of narrative developed a two-person system (first and third).

2 *Verbal tenses in* RD

The problem of the difference between DN and DC in the system of verbal tenses is more complicated than that of grammatical persons. Generally, DN can be considered oriented toward 'epic', i.e. past time; it renders past actions.[13] Therefore, the basic tense of DN in Czech is the past (preterit). The usage of the so-called historical present does not substantially change matters; historical present is a special stylistic device, the effect of which is based on the contrast between present form and preterit function (determined by context). The basic orientation of DN toward past tense is not thereby affected. It is important to note that in DN, tense cannot be used as a shifter; both past tense and historical present are used absolutely.

In contrast, in DC the usage of verbal tenses is based on a different principle. The tense here expresses the reference to the individual and the shifting time position of the speaker, the speaking character. The temporal position of the speaker, i.e. the moment of the delivery of his utterance, the speaker's 'now' (the *origo* in Karl Bühler's terminology) represents the time centre, in relation to which the use of verbal tenses (as well as other means of time *deixis*) is determined. In other words, verbal tenses in DC, like the grammatical persons, are shifters, with the following simple rules governing their usage in Czech: The present tense is used to express actions simultaneous with the time position of the speaker; the past tense,

13 'What is depicted by the epic poet is not the present but the past.' (K. Friedemann, *Die Rolle des Erzählers in der Epik*, Leipzig, 1910, p. 99.)

actions anterior to the moment of speaking; and future tense, those which are posterior to that moment.[14]

In many languages RD is characterized by a form of past tense; this fact, again, can be interpreted as RD's formal identification with DN. The analysis of Czech RD, however, reveals a rather curious situation. According to the traditional view, Czech RD has 'the same tense as ... the direct or indirect discourse [would have] in the same context',[15] i.e., the present, preterit and future operate as shifters. This statement holds true for many – perhaps for the majority of – instances of Czech RD. The following examples illustrate this usage of tenses:

19/ *Present* VLACH: Of course Gamza *is entitled* to critical freedom in all his theatrical columns. Vlach *is* not *intending* to interfere with this right of his. [PF]

20/ *Preterit* JURA: They *had been betrayed* and *had* to be killed. Nikola *had* to be killed. [ON]

21/ *Future* ŠIMON: He *will bring* his laundry as soon as possible. [VF]

In modern Czech prose, however, numerous instances of RD can be found which reveal a different pattern: preterit (past tense) is used here absolutely, i.e. for expressing any action without discriminating between present, past and future. The short dialogue quoted below is an extremely instructive example: The question expressed in DD uses the present, whereas in the answer expressed in RD the preterit occurs, though the action is also 'present', i.e. simultaneous with the 'now' of the speaker:

22/ NIKOLA: 'Is father out in the fields?'
 MOTHER: No, he *was* home ... [ON]

In most cases, RD with absolute past tense can be found in interior monologues:

23/ STANISLAV: Ah, darkness *was* just right for what he *wanted* to ask her. [PP]

 MOTHER: So this *was* her Růža. ... This *was* her Růženka, whom she used to take pride in. [PL]

---

14 In some languages the system of tenses makes it possible to express additional nuances of the time-orientation of verbal action; however, the basic principle of tense functions is not affected thereby in any essential way.
15 Haller, p. 122.

It would be tempting to speculate whether the past-tense type is the original form of RD in Czech or whether it came later under the influence of translations from Western literature.[16] This question, however, can be answered only by a thorough historical investigation which I do not intend to undertake here. I would venture to say only that the intensive use of RD in dialogue, so typical of modern fiction, has reinforced the position of the first type of RD (with three shifting tenses).[17]

Two different systems of tenses (present, preterit, future used as shifters *versus* preterit used absolutely) represent a highly important fact to be accounted for by the theory of RD. It is another indication of the transitional character of RD within the framework of the opposition of DC and DN. Whereas the first type of Czech RD coincides in its tense system and usage with DC (showing the positive value of this discriminative feature), the second type is identical (in the negative value of the feature) with DN. Apparently, RD enjoys a certain 'free space' in which it can fluctuate toward either of the two poles of DN and DC. This flexibility is an essential quality of the device which, as will be seen, provides a base for a substantial transformation of RD in modern fiction.

3 Deixis in RD

The speaker's control in DC accounts for the fact that characters' speeches are anchored in an extralinguistic situation; they are situational.[18] The situation of a DC utterance is defined by the time and space position of its speaker-character. Some demonstrative means (pronouns, adverbs) assume the function of pointing to the shifting time-space position of the speaking character; this function (Bühler's *demonstratio ad oculos*) will be called *deixis*. By implication, demonstrative means with deictic function behave as shifters.

On the contrary, DN with no speaker's control cannot be linked to an extralinguistic situation; it is a nonsituational discourse. Therefore, no

16 Cf. J. Křesálková, 'Polopřímá řeč a nebezpečí, které v sobě skrývá pro překladatele' [Represented Discourse and its Pitfalls for Translators], *Dialog*, I, no. 1 (1957), pp. 18–42.

17 The system of tenses in RD also represents an interesting topic for comparative literature study. As already indicated, English, German and French RD are said to be characterized by various forms of past tense. The Russian RD, apparently, is similar to the Czech RD; according to Kovtunova, Russian RD employs the same system of tenses as direct discourse, at the same time, however, 'it can exist in the past tense, and in that case it is more difficult to identify.' (Kovtunova, p. 21–2.)

18 This holds true especially for dialogue; see J. Mukařovský, 'Dialog a monolog' [Dialogue and Monologue] in *Kapitoly z české poetiky* [Chapters from Czech Poetics], Prague, 1948, vol. I, p. 133ff.

pointing to the external situation, no *demonstratio ad oculos* is possible in DN. Demonstrative means in DN do not behave as shifters expressing *deixis*; rather, they point to some spatial or temporal centres of the narrated action, fulfilling a function which can be called *elenxis*.[19]

The function of *elenxis* is, however, possible also within DC; therefore, only *deixis* operates as a discriminative text feature. We will say that the feature assumes positive value in DC when some demonstrative means acquire the function of shifting *deixis*; it shows a negative value in DN where no deictic function of demonstrative means is possible.[20] If, from this standpoint, we turn our attention to RD, we find that demonstrative means with deictic function, behaving as shifters with reference to the time-space position of the speaker, are a marked feature of its verbal structure.

a) Spatial *deixis*. The basic means of spatial *deixis* in Czech RD are adverbs, like *zde, tady, tu, tuhle* (all of them meaning 'here' with various stylistic connotations), *sem* ('hither'), *tam* ('there'), *odtud* ('thither'), *tudy* ('this way'), etc. Moreover, demonstrative pronouns like *ten* ('that'), *tento* ('this'), *tenhle* ('this here'), etc., can fulfill the same function.

24/ NIKOLA: Should he wait until Volová or Chust where his situation will be much worse than *here*? [ON]

25/ SOLDIER: Could they phone from *here* to get a truck or at least a motorcycle to go *there*, to *that* place? [VF]

26/ ŠIMON: But, good heavens, he can't in any case get home *this way*; the path is flooded. [VF]

27/ ŠIMON: *That* creek appears to be his creek, and it will take him downstream straight home. [VF]

28/ GAMZA: Mrs. Torgler has undoubtedly seen *this* certificate several times already ... [PF]

b) Temporal *deixis*. The basic means of temporal *deixis* are various adverbs or adverbial phrases; their use in RD is illustrated by the following examples:

19 See Vinogradov's analysis of narrative 'dating' in his essay 'Stil' Pikovoj damy' [Style of the Queen of Spades] in *Puškin. Vremennik Puškinskoj komissii AN SSSR*, Moscow – Leningrad, 1936, vol. II, pp. 74–147.
20 In general terms, the double function of demonstrative means (*topologiques*) was described by A.J. Greimas: One type is characterized 'by relationship to the situation of communication, another constructs a net of relations with respect to a certain objective deixis' ('Les topologiques', *Cahiers de lexicologie*, IV (1964), I, p. 28.)

29/ NIKOLA: Or had [the magic branch] worked only during the war and *now* was its power all gone? [ON]

30/ ROSENSTAM: Did the spinners fired from their job visit Miss Kazmar *today?* [PP]

31/ SOLDIER: *Last April* they got it from a bomb, and not a trace of them was found. [VF]

32/ BEER: At last! *Tomorrow* or *the day after tomorrow,* he will go to Peter Šuhaj. [ON]

The examples quoted are sufficient to illustrate the nature and role of *deixis* in Czech RD. It is obvious that *deixis* pointing to an extralinguistic situation is possible in RD; deictic means have the nature of shifters. Thus, the presence of *deixis* becomes an important feature of RD. RD shares the positive value of this feature with DC and is differentiated by it from DN.

4 Allocution in RD

A characteristic feature of DC utterances is the fact that the function of allocution (Bühler's *Appel*) can be expressed by some of their verbal means. According to Bühler, *Appel* is a signal to the listener intended to 'govern his intrinsic or extrinsic behaviour'.[21] Allocution presupposes a listener and therefore it is proper to dialogic utterances (which compose the basic ingredient of DC). It is, however, also typical of 'soliloquy' (another basic type of utterance in DC); here allocution assumes a specific character, that of addressing oneself. The allocutional function in DC is expressed by certain allocutional means, the most important of which in Czech are imperative mood, interrogative sentence and the vocative case as a means of address.[22]

In contrast, DN has no allocutional function inasmuch as it is, by definition, utterance without hearer. Therefore, allocutional means are incompatible with the structure of DN.[23]

If we investigate allocution in RD, we discover that RD utterances can

21 Bühler, *Sprachtheorie*, p. 28.
22 An analysis of allocutional means is offered in A.V. Isačenko's essay 'O prizyvnoj funkcii jazyka' [On the Allocutional Function of Language] in *Recueil linguistique de Bratislava*, Bratislava, 1948, pp. 45–57.
23 As with some other verbal means which will be discussed, allocutional means can be found occasionally in concrete manifestations of the traditional type; they result from the influence of the rhetorical mode of narrative; for more about rhetorical narrative, see here, pp. 59–65, 104–6.

express allocutional function. At the same time, however, allocutional means in Czech RD display some specific modifications in form.

a) Imperative. The system of grammatical persons in RD (no second person!) does not allow the use of the regular formation of Czech imperative (with the second person as its basic form). Instead, the so-called analytic (periphrastic) imperative, using the third person indicative plus a particle (*ať, nechť*) is used:

33/ VÁCLAV: Jarmila shall also thank her. Madam was so kind. ... [PPr]

34/ GREAT-GRANDMOTHER: Nella shall make sure whether Grandma covered up the lamp. [PF]

The effect of these sentences is different from that of sentences with the regular imperative form. We could say that the appeal is expressed in a 'muted', 'veiled' manner because in Czech this form is typical more of request than of command.

b) Interrogative sentences. The fundamental type of interrogative sentence is to be classified as allocutional means since 'every question presupposes an answer, i.e., a certain reaction, in this case a verbal one'.[24] Besides allocutional function, however, a question may also have modal or emotive functions. These functions are dominant in deliberative and rhetorical questions which, as a matter of fact, do not presuppose any answer.

This distinction is very important for the theory of RD. Questions requiring answers are relatively rare in RD. In earlier Czech prose, they often had the form of dependent (subordinate) sentences.[25] In modern fiction, syntactically independent RD questions can be found, their 'allocutionality', however, as with imperative sentences, is 'muted', because of the prohibition of the second person of the verb:

35/ BEER: Could Jasinko bring him about four wagonloads of timber? [ON]

36/ NELLA: But where did Grandma throw the burning match? [PF]

In contrast to this rare type of question, deliberative and rhetorical questions belong to the most frequent means of RD. However, because of their basically emotive function, they will be discussed in the next section.

c) Address. Direct address in the vocative case does not exist in Czech RD;

24 Isačenko, p. 50.   25 Trávníček, vol. II, p. 750.

RD address is expressed in the nominative. Thus, again, an effect of indirect, 'veiled' address results:

37/ ROSENSTAM: Does *Miss Kazmar* know that the protest meeting against the firing at Kazmar's was originally called at Úly? [PF]

38/ DEFENCE COUNSEL: Torgler's mother had arrived; would *the presiding judge* allow her to be present at the session? [PF]

These instances, however, are ambiguous. Formally, nominative address coalesces with explicit naming of the hearer which is often used in RD as a substitute for the lack of the second person. We will return to this phenomenon later in more detail (see pp. 51–2).

An analysis of allocution in Czech RD reveals again the basic quality of RD, its transitional nature. In the feature of allocution, this principle can be seen reflected in the following way: By the very possibility of allocution, RD goes with DC; at the same time, however, usage of allocutional means is different from that in DC – some means are different in form (imperative, address), some in frequency (questions). These formal modifications of allocutional means, implied by the system of grammatical persons in RD, bring RD closer to DN in this discriminative feature. This being so, allocution and allocutional means contribute to the intrinsic tensions which characterize RD as a stylistic device.

5 *Emotive function in* RD

According to R. Jakobson, emotive function 'aims a direct expression of the speaker's attitude toward what he is speaking about. It tends to produce an impression of a certain emotion whether true or feigned'.[26] The fact that DN does not express any reference to the speaker implies that it does not possess emotive function and does not use emotive means.[27] In contrast, DC commonly does express various subjective attitudes of the speaking characters by a variety of emotive means.

As far as RD is concerned, we can say that emotive function and means expressing it are most characteristic of its features. The most primitive emotive means to be found in RD are interjections.[28] Although their role in

26 'Linguistics and Poetics' in T. A. Sebeok (ed.), *Style in Language*, Cambridge, Mass., 1960, p. 354.

27 Instances of emotive means found in DN in some manifestations of the traditional type are 'deviances' from the DN model. They are either devices or rhetoric, or first signs of developing RD; see my analysis in *O stylu moderní české prózy*, p. 36.

28 I have in mind 'expressive' not 'allocutional' interjections; for the distinction, see Isačenko, p. 55.

the verbal structure of RD is minor, they can be, in indistinct instances, an important index of the device:

39/ DOCTOR: *Ugh!* He would much sooner meet him here again on the dissecting-table than in Chust. [ON]

Another means of emotive function – the exclamatory sentence – occurs with great frequency in RD. Bally and Lips have already pointed to exclamatory sentences as one feature indicating the presence of RD in the context of narrative. Exclamatory sentences are a standard device especially of RD interior monologues (example 40), but can be found in dialogues as well (example 41):

40/ ONDŘEJ: The fire-proof curtain! Why didn't they remember it before! ... How often Ondřej had pulled it down! [PP]

41/ NELLA: They can afford liquor, but they can't afford milk! They can afford gas, but they can't afford shoes! Isn't this a topsy-turvy world! [PP]

Another means of emotive syntax – the optative sentence – is also quite common in RD:

42/ PEOPLE: Oh, if only they also could take from the rich and give to the poor! If only they could take revenge for injustice too! [ON]

Deliberative and rhetorical questions can be included among the means of emotive function, as already indicated; they are very frequent in RD:[29]

43/ NIKOLA: Is something going on? Is Eržika going to fly away? Yes, something is going on. [ON]

44/ ONDŘEJ: What will she do when he tells her that he's going to leave her? Will she flutter her eye-lashes, turn pale, and will her hands tremble as they did on that Christmas drive to Nechleby? [PP]

All our investigations have stressed the fact that emotive means are rather frequent in RD; this frequency reflects the generally emotive character of interior monologues expressed in RD.

29 Referring to these kinds of questions, W. Hoffmeister states: 'The most frequent form of RD is question.' (*Studien zur erlebten Rede bei Thomas Mann und Robert Musil,* The Hague, 1965, p. 39.)

6 Semantic features of RD

An analysis of discriminative features 1 to 5 has revealed that verbal means exist which, by their 'additional' textual qualities, differentiate DC from DN. Proceeding now to the investigation of semantic differences between DC and DN, we will again seek out verbal means (or systems of verbal means) which can carry the discriminative features of semantic distinction. In this case, however, isolating individual verbal means would be rather inefficient. The semantics of DC and DN is a 'contextual' semantics, i.e., those planes are semantically differentiated only as contextual wholes. Individual semantic means (for example, words) participate in the formation of that contextual semantics, and, at the same time, acquire specific semantic qualities by the impact of context. In isolated semantic means, these qualities cannot be observed.

Contextual semantics is an almost untouched problem, though some general observations about it have been made. Thus, for example, J. Mukařovský when analysing the semantics of dialogue described it as an alternation of different 'semantic contexts' and pointed to some linguistic means which contribute to expressing the semantic distinction.[30] V.V. Vinogradov, characterizing the 'dramatic word' (modes of expression in drama), observed that it renders 'not only differences in reality, but also differences in the view-points of the acting characters'.[31] Only recently, A.J. Greimas set up a theoretical framework for the study of contextual semantics, by distinguishing in semantic units invariant semantic 'nucleus' and variable semantic components generated by the context.[32]

Generalizing these observations, we can say that an utterance (be it a monologue or part of a dialogue) represents an idiosyncratic, subjective semantic context in the sense that – besides its referential semantics – it expresses attitudes, viewpoints and evaluations of its speaker-originator. The speaker is the primary factor organizing and controlling the contextual semantics of his utterance.

Relating this statement to our general problem, we are reminded that in the verbal structure of narrative prose only DC utterances are under the speaker's control. Therefore, only in DC, idiosyncratic, subjective semantic qualities, reflecting the individual viewpoints and attitudes of the speaking characters, are created. Subjective contextual semantics is one of the most important discriminative features of DC. In contrast, DN (i.e., that model of DN which our investigation is based on) has a 'zero' contextual semantics.

30 Mukařovský, *Kapitoly*, vol. I, p. 134f.
31 V.V. Vinogradov, *Stiľ Puškina* [Pushkin's Style], Moscow, 1941, p. 86.
32 A.J. Greimas, *Sémantique structurale*, Paris, 1966, esp. p. 50ff.

As we know, DN is assumed to reveal no reference to the speaker-narrator. This implies that no individual attitudes, no point of view, no subjective semantics is present in DN; it produces the effect of an anonymous and impartial report.

When we investigate RD against the background of this opposition, we discover that in semantic aspect it is identical with DC, i.e., that its verbal means carry the contextual component of subjective semantics. This fact has been generally apprehended in some descriptions of RD. Thus, for example, Ch. Bally speaks about a 'context feature' of RD which consists in the fact that ideas and feelings expressed in RD are 'incompatible with the narrator-reporter'; they can be interpreted only when related to a character. Fr. Trávníček observed about an example of RD: 'What is narrative and what is RD can be distinguished by the sense.'[33] When expressed in our terminology, these observations have the same meaning: the semantics of RD is the subjective semantics of fictional characters, and RD thus shares a discriminative feature of DC, distinguishing it from DN.

We will try to analyse this semantic feature of RD in more detail and in some systematic way; however, with regard to our present knowledge of the contextual semantics of discourse, no definite results and classification schemes can be promised.

1 Attitudinal semantics

The basic component of the subjective semantics of RD is the expression of individual attitudes and evaluations relating to the verbalized thoughts, depicted actions, characters, etc. Attitudinal semantics employs as its means primarily qualifying adjectives and adverbs, carrying the speaker's evaluation of an object or action. Some examples:

45/ SVOZIL on ERŽIKA: She's amazingly *sweet*. [ON]

46/ NELLA: But she would be embarrassed to death before another man, who is, besides, such a close friend and such a *good* man. [PP]

47/ JUDGE: Dimitrov misuses the defendant's dock as a platform for *destructive* Marxist slogans. [PF]

48/ NIKOLA: How could he live so *miserably* and *deplorably* when he has a magic branch in his hand? [ON]

It is obvious that the attitudes and evaluations expressed by the pertinent adjectives and adverbs are subjective and idiosyncratic; they can, but

33 Bally, *GRM* VI (1914), p. 420; Trávníček, vol. II, p. 138.

need not, be shared by other characters. The lexical meaning of these qualifying expressions is focused in such a direction as to contribute to building up of the subjective semantics of the RD context. In some cases, attitudinal meaning is combined with emotive connotation which emphasizes the positive or negative evaluation originating with the speaking character:

49/ DOORMAN: *Damn* foreigners! A German would never do that. [PF]

50/ ŠIMON: Now he need not to go into that *rotten* business at all. [VF]

Besides adjectives and adverbs, some substantives are able to express personal attitudes and relationships. One such group is made up of terms of kinship, such as *otec* ('father'), *táta* ('daddy'), *matka* ('mother'), *máma* ('mommy') *žena* ('wife'), *muž* ('husband'), *dcera* ('daughter'), *syn* ('son'), etc. There are numerous examples of the use of these semantic markers in Czech RD; here, I will quote two of them only:

51/ JURA: *Father* will also flee. He will take the livestock to the meadows, leave *mother* with the small children there, and he himself will go to Poland or to Roumania. [ON]

52/ INNKEEPER: Under such circumstances, he would, of course, be happy to read the book; he and his *wife* and his boys, too. [VF]

Hypocoristic names and nicknames represent another group of means which can be used to express the personal relationship of one speaking character to another:

53/ ONDŘEJ: *Liduška* said something to the effect that he was in a madhouse. [PP]

Family and kinship expressions are conspicuous means of subjective semantics; however, in a subjective semantic context any noun can contribute to the expression of personal attitudes, either positive or negative. Thus, for example, in Ivan Olbracht's *Nikola Šuhaj, Robber*, Šuhaj is called *Nikolka*, or *sokol Nikola* ('falcon Nikola') in RD expressing collective monologues of the people; whereas in RD utterances of the policemen, he is *bandita* ('bandit'), *vrah* ('murderer'), *loupežník* ('robber'), *zločinec* ('criminal'). Those designations, reflecting radically opposite attitudes, contribute in a substantial way to the formation of subjective contextual semantics marking RD utterances.

Quite often, 'attitudinal' nouns can be reinforced by a positive or negative emotive connotation:

54/ DOCTOR: He let himself become spellbound by the name of Nikola Šuhaj, just like all those *fools* around here. [ON]

55/ GREAT-GRANDMOTHER: Of course, Nella will side with that *nincompoop!* [PF]

56/ ONDŘEJ: What might *that poor thing* be doing now? [PP]

The groups of adjectives, adverbs and nouns cited represent only a token of means of attitudinal subjective semantics; a more detailed analysis would doubtless reveal other, more refined means of this kind.

2 Modality

By modality we mean here that evaluation of the verbal action which attributes to it the quality of reality, unreality, possibility, conditionality, desirability, or necessity. Modality is distinguished both from attitudinal semantics and from emotivity. Analyzing modality in RD, we come to the conclusion that RD is marked by a subjective modality, i.e., the modal status of verbal actions is here controlled by the decision of a speaker, in accordance with the general trends of his subjective semantics. Again, in this respect, RD coincides with DC and differs from DN. Here is a very good example illustrating the point, a direct clash between the modality of RD and that of DN:

57/ ŠIMON: (RD:) That creek appears to be his creek and it will take him downstream straight home. (DN:) In a quarter of an hour he got out of the forest and stood before Dolina, but in a quite different place; it was a different creek. [VF]

As in the case of attitudinal semantics, subjective modality is not expressed by basic meaning of modal means; modal means and their basic functions[34] are 'neutral' with respect to the semantic opposition of DC and DN. Subjective modality is an accessory textual quality by virtue of which the modal evaluation is attributable to a speaker; only in the context of the discourse as a whole can such attribution be expressed and identified.

34 For a classification of modal means in standard Czech see: M. Dokulil, 'K modální výstavbě věty' [On the Modal Structure of Sentence] in *Studie a práce lingvistické,* Prague, 1954, vol. I, pp. 255–62.

In other words, modality becomes a discriminative feature of RD only where we can determine from the context that modal evaluation originates with a character, that it expresses a character's view of the rendered events. The following examples, in my opinion, illustrate the case:

a) The verbal action is considered real from the subjective viewpoint of a character:

58/ NIKOLA: God's power is in him. And it will not betray him. [ON]

59/ GAMZA: Gamza will not get to the defence, that's clear. [PF]

b) The verbal action is considered possible or likely from the viewpoint of a character:

60/ CAPTAIN: Oh, the cowards! Obviously, they didn't want to find them! Obviously, it suited them that the bandits constantly changed their location. [ON]

61/ RŮŽENA: Maybe she'll learn something about Karel from that frog. [PP]

c) The verbal action is considered conditional from the viewpoint of a character:

62/ ERŽIKA: If it's the Majdan witch who said it, then it's true. [ON]

d) The verbal action is considered desirable, necessary, needed, etc., from the viewpoint of a character:

63/ ŠIMON: He can't keep still; at the very least he must make a comment. [VF]

64/ BRYCH: To put it simply, he doesn't long for it; he just wants peace of mind for his work, and nothing more. [OC]

The semantic features of Czech RD, just exemplified, and all others that might be discovered by further analysis (for example, subjective causality) can be described on special groups of verbal means, which are able to acquire contextual semantic components in a text controlled by the speaker. These components point to a speaking character as their source; they are subject to semantic shifts depending on the changes of speakers. It is only the contextual components which represent the discriminative feature of DC. In DN, the same semantic means can be used but without the contextual components.

To make the point more explicit, let us observe the following transformation:

(DC) A: 'B is my sister.' → (DN) B is A's sister.

In the first case, 'sister' carries a semantic component referring to the 'outside' (extra-textual) speaker; in the second case, the meaning of 'sister' is specified with respect to a text-inherent modifier. Thus, the situation appears quite similar to the distinction of *deixis* and *elenxis*. Semantic means with contextual components are speaker-oriented (deictic), whereas those without the component are context-oriented (elenctic). RD is characterized by contextual speaker-oriented semantic components. Thus, it conforms in this discriminative feature with DC and differs from DN.

7 *Speech-level features in* RD

We can expect that DC utterances, controlled by an individualized speaker, will make use of verbal means reflecting the speaker's idiolect; these means will be especially conspicuous if the speaker's idiolect is based on a substandard speech level (on a social or regional dialect). This expectation is usually fulfilled in the traditional narrative text, where particular characters are differentiated by the so-called speech characterization (cf. here, p. 94). On the contrary, DN is assumed to be based on a 'neutral' speech level reflecting the standard language of the period.

As far as speech-level features are concerned, RD is generally identical with DC. Thus, for example, 'loose' structures of colloquial syntax[35] are quite frequent in Czech RD:

65/ KAZMAR: Freeways, that's what the Manager envied them. [PP]

66/ TEACHER: He is the local teacher, a one-room school – he was just about to get married, they had the furniture already – her name was Anežka. [VF]

On the base of colloquial syntax, lexical means of colloquial language, of slang or of jargon are often used as idiosyncratic means of speech characterization. Thus, for example, the RD utterances of Růžena in the trilogy by M. Pujmanová contain elements of upper-class jargon characterizing the speech of a *parvenu*:

35 For a description of these structures in contemporary Czech see: A. Jedlička, 'K charakteristice syntaxe současné spisovné češtiny' [Some Features of Syntax of Contemporary Standard Czech], *Slavica Pragensia*, x (Acta Universitatis Carolinae, Philologica 1–3, 1968), p. 149f.

67 RŮŽENA – RÓ: But Mrs. Ró wishes something *highly fashionable*; she's already said so. [PF]

In other instances, idiosyncratic means originate rather in bookish layers of standard language, for example, in juristic jargon:

68/ JUDGE: The presiding judge is rather interested in knowing how much of *the said* fuel was needed to set fire to a large hall. [PF]

Though elements of idiosyncratic style are quite common in RD, their discriminatory power is rather limited. This holds true especially for modern fiction where the speech-level differentiation, typical for the traditional text, is generally abolished (cf. here, 96).

Perhaps we should bring this analysis of the verbal features of Czech RD to a close here and try to come to some general conclusions. It has been shown that RD combines in a specific manner discriminative features of DN with those of DC. Its essential grammatical feature (system of grammatical persons) is identical with that of DN; in other features, it is (or, at least, can be) identical with DC; some of the DC features are formally modified in RD. Table 1 following summarizes the opposition between DC and DN expressed in terms of discriminative features; it also indicates the transitional position of RD. Again in this table, 0 symbolizes the negative value of the feature, 1 its positive value, 1/0 positive or negative.

The table shows how positive and negative values of discriminative features participate in the verbal structure of RD. At the same time, it reveals that RD has no discriminative features of its own. RD *is, rather, a certain concentration of some positive* (DC) *features emerging on the unspecified* (*'zero'*) *base of* DN. The degree of establishment and, consequently, the certainty of RD's identification in fictional texts, depends fully on the conspicuousness of the features of DC employed and on the degree of their concentration. This *transitional* and *contextual* character makes RD one of the most flexible devices of modern fiction, leaving writers a high degree of freedom for developing their own, idiosyncratic modifications and variations of RD. This holds true perhaps even more about the functions of RD in modern fictional structure, as will become evident in the following section.

II FUNCTIONS OF RD IN MODERN CZECH FICTION

There is a tradition in the study of RD which has identified RD with interior monologue, with that form of characters' speech which became the dominant device of the modern psychological novel, satisfying its need for a

Table 1

Discriminative Features / Mode of Characters' Speech	system of persons	system of tenses	deixis	allocution	emotive function	subjective semantics	specified speech level
DN	0	0	0	0	0	0	0
RD	0	0/1	1	1*	1	1	1
DC	1	1	1	1	1	1	1

(*with formal modifications)

direct self-revelation of characters' mental states and processes. The identification of RD with interior monologue is, however, based on rather limited evidence; only in its first stages of development was RD used exclusively for the expression of interior monologues. Recent investigations of RD, based on its usage in modern fiction, have revealed beyond any doubt that both basic forms of characters' speech, interior monologue and dialogue, can be found expressed in RD.[36]

Thus, from the functional point of view, RD can be considered a device synonymous with direct discourse (DD) and unmarked direct discourse (UDD).[37] These devices can be said to be competing for the same functions of expressing dialogues and interior monologues of fictional characters; therefore, an investigation of functions of RD has to be set in the wider framework of an investigation of the functional competition between RD, DD and UDD.

If we characterize the three devices as synonymous from the general functional viewpoint, we do not deny certain differences in their effects, resulting from their formal differences. It was precisely the existence of these differences which led to speculations about some general trends in the competition of RD and DD. M. Lips suggests that portions of characters' speech which are semantically less important usually have the form of RD, whereas those which are semantically more important are found expressed in DD. On the other hand, L. Spitzer believes that the selection of devices is influenced primarily by factors of emotive nature: speeches of a high emotive status are in DD, speeches emotionally 'muted' tend to be expressed in RD.

My investigation of RD in modern Czech prose indicates that both semantic and emotive factors can influence the selection of RD or DD. At the same time, however, I arrived at the conclusion that other factors, especially idiosyncratic preferences of the author are at work which make the situation in functional employment of the investigated devices rather complicated. With regard to that complexity, general functions of DD, UDD and RD can be formulated only in probabilistic terms:

1 Direct discourse is the usual, primary means of expressing dialogue in modern Czech fiction (as it has been in the traditional type); moreover, in rare cases, it is used to express a specific kind of interior monologue.

2 Unmarked direct discourse is used most often to express interior mono-

36 See esp.: Anne G. Landry, *Represented Discourse in the Novels of François Mauriac*, Washington, DC, 1953; L. Doležel, *O stylu moderní české prózy*, Prague, 1960; Hoffmeister, footnote 29.

37 Unmarked DD (UDD) is a variant of DD which preserves all the grammatical, semantic and speech-level features of DD, but lacks its demarcation marks (the conventional punctuation of DD).

logues; some specific types of dialogue can also be found occasionally expressed by this device.

3 Represented discourse became the most common, primary device of expressing interior monologue in modern Czech fiction; at the same time, dialogues can be found expressed in RD quite often. In harmony with its form, RD developed a specific function of its own – expressing dialogues and monologues of a narrative character.

As this outline of general functions has indicated already, primary and secondary functions are to be distinguished. The primary function of DD is expression of dialogue, that of UDD and RD, expression of interior monologue. As their secondary functions, DD expresses a specific kind of interior monologue, UDD and RD some specific kinds of dialogue. A specific secondary function of RD is expressing narrative dialogues and interior monologues. Both in their primary and secondary functions, DD is in opposition to RD; in contrast, UDD, though formally almost identical with DD, in its functions is rather close to RD.

There is no need for extensive documentation of the primary functions; examples of them can be easily found on every page of a modern fictional text. For the sake of illustration, let us give one example for each device and function:

a) DD in dialogue:

69/ 'There were some – rumours,' murmured Juraj. 'About you ... and about him. ... Things can't go on like this, Polana.'
    'Why?' burst out Polana sharply. 'Because of those stupid rumours?' [čH]

b) UDD in interior monologue:

70/ Why hasn't that youngster been drafted yet, thought Nikola, a feeling of anger seizing him, he's only a year younger than I am and he's seventeen already! [ON]

c) RD expressing interior monologue:

71/ HORDUBAL: This used to be Hordubal's field? It was, without a doubt – all stones, they said, and yet Pjosa had a crop of barley here, he's got potatoes here, and a little patch of flax; see, how Pjosa's field and Hordubal's field have been joined together. [čH]

More interesting is the study of the instances where the devices appear in their secondary functions. As far as DD is concerned, in modern fiction it

rarely can be found in its secondary function, i.e., expressing interior monologue. Apparently, DD is too definite, unambiguous and compact, thus dis-
playing qualities which make it unsuitable for modern 'chaotic' interior
monologue. It is used only where a definite, clear and usually rather short
thought-remark is to be verbalized:

72/ A few words flashed through his (Nikola's) head: 'Nothing can happen to
me. I have such power from God.' [ON]

Interior monologue of this kind preserves the form and style of that in
older fiction. The development of modern interior monologue, however, is
connected with the use of RD, and UDD, which, by their form, are much
better suited for its specific structure, style and effect.

UDD can be found quite frequently in its secondary function, expressing
certain specific types of dialogue. For example, it is used to express dialogues which are unimportant, incidental, or speeches uttered by unimportant, episodic characters. In this case, UDD, apparently, takes over a
typical function of indirect discourse:

73/ [Prokop] went to the Inquiry Office of the police. Jiří Tomeš, the dusty clerk
flipped through his books, the engineer Tomeš Jiří; that, if you please, is such-
and-such a street in Smíchov. It was obviously an old address. Nevertheless,
Prokop dashed over to such-and-such a street in Smíchov. The house-porter
shook his head when asked about Jiří Tomeš. A person answering that description used to live here, over a year ago; where he is living now, nobody
knows. [ČK]

Another special type of dialogue, quite often expressed by UDD, is fragmentary dialogue. A good example of it is a telephone conversation verbalized in such a way that only what one participant says is expressed:

74/ Brych here! I have been hunting for you for an hour ... your wife's time has
come ... yes, I got a doctor, everything is in order ... no, keep calm, everything's going well ... [OC]

RD can be found competing with UDD in examples such as those given
above and in similar cases;[38] this confirms the functional kinship of the two

---

38 As a matter of fact, UDD in example 73, as well as in some other instances, was interpreted by a translator of Čapek's *Krakatit* as RD (Macmillan edition, New York, 1925);
he translated the Czech present by the English past tense.

devices. At the same time, however, RD acquired a specific secondary function, a function for which it is best suited by its form: expressing dialogues
and interior monologues of a narrative nature. Dialogues and monologues
of this kind can be said to verbalize actions, episodes, incidents which usually do not belong to the main action. Thus, for example, M. Pujmanová
in *Playing with Fire* often uses RD to express narrative testimonies at the
Leipzig trial:

75/ GOEBBELS: The leading men of the party assembled in Berlin for a political
session, as was necessary from time to time so that the national socialists
maintained a united front in the election campaign. ... The Führer was just
dining at his place and the table conversation was, as usual, lively and cordial,
when the host was called to the phone. Doctor Hanfstängel, head of the press
service, was phoning to tell him that Parliament was burning. [PF]

Without doubt, this function of RD arises from its formal identity with
DN, the basic form of introducing action motifs. Such episodes, as given in
the preceding example, can be compared to the 'stories within the story'
which are typical of older fiction. However, when expressed in RD they do
not disturb the smooth flow of narrative, being formally assimilated into
DN.

The availability of a whole system of devices for expressing characters'
utterances, gave rise to dialogues and interior monologues formally heterogeneous, i.e., expressed by more than one device. In older fiction with its
repertoire limited to DD, there was no possibility of formally differentiating
segments of a dialogue or interior monologue; the whole speech was formally homogeneous, expressed throughout in DD. In modern fiction, formally
heterogeneous dialogues and interior monologues became quite a common
phenomenon.

It is obvious that formal heterogeneity cannot be materialized without
'violating' the general functional tendencies. Evidence shows that in many
cases such a 'violation' results from the impact of semantic and/or emotive
factors. In other words, formal differentiation reflects a semantic and/or
emotive differentiation of various segments of a dialogue or interior monologue.

This is rather obvious in the most conspicuous and very old example of
heterogeneous speech, in the dialogue consisting of a question expressed in
DD and an answer expressed in RD:[39]

39 W. Bühler found rare examples of short answers expressed in RD even in the eigh-
teenth-century English novel (*Die 'erlebte Rede' im englischen Roman*, Schweizer
anglistische Studien, vol. IV, pp. 35, 61).

76/ PROSECUTOR: 'Janitor, when you opened parliament gate number five for Torgler, didn't you notice a peculiar smell coming from him?' ... No he, the janitor, did not observe anything on deputy Torgler when he was leaving Parliament shortly after eight. [PF]

The use of DD in questions is obviously conditioned by its verbal features, especially by its ability to use the grammatical second person and to express allocution directly. On the other hand, the answer usually has a narrative character – it is a short episode. By its very form, RD is especially suited, as indicated above, to expressing that type of speech.

Formal differentiation within the question-answer dialogue is only one of many possibilities of segmenting a dialogue into formally differentiated portions. There is no need to go into detail here, besides noticing that formal differentiation can be observed not only on the frontier between speeches belonging to different participants, but even within the limits of one speech:

77/ FATHER: 'Go home and change into more civilized dress,' he ordered, 'and hurry up!' He will wait for her here. They will go for a short walk together. [PPr]

The shift in the form of this speech (DD – RD) can be explained by factors of emotive nature: direct allocution (order) prefers DD; the statement is expressed in RD. At the same time, this short example illustrates the complexity of functional employment of devices of characters' speech. In the second part of the speech (expressed in RD), the general functional tendency demanding DD in dialogue does not apply. Instead, the emotive factor becomes dominant requiring formal differentiation between the emotive climax (order) and anticlimax (statement).

At this point it is worth noting (though it somehow transcends the scope of this work) that the use of several different devices of characters' speech in one dialogue (or even within one speech of a dialogue), testifies to the fact that modern fictional dialogue has acquired features which make it a specific form, distinct from both everyday (communicative) and dramatic dialogue. Modern fictional dialogue developed its specific forms and functions which cannot be explained by referring to other, nonfictional types of dialogue. The theory of dialogue in fiction is to be embodied primarily in the framework of a general theory of narrative structure, describing forms and functions of dialogue with reference to other basic components of the structure, namely narrative and interior monologue.

This general observation is true also of modern interior monologue which has become the most prominent specific component of fictional structure; drama and 'everyday speech' have nothing to compare with modern interior monologue, either in variety or in complexity of forms, styles and effects.

In its formal structure, interior monologue follows some of the patterns observed in dialogue. For one thing, formal heterogeneity has become a common feature of its structure; quite often, one monologue is expressed by more than one alternating device:

78/ JARMILA: Why do they meddle in all her affairs? After all, they have no idea what life actually is. What do I have in common with them? I am only I. And is it possible that she used to play 'Parcheesi' with these boys? [PPr]

In this example, UDD surrounded by segments of RD (RD – UDD – RD) brings into prominence the emotive climax of the monologue. In cases like this, the role of form as carrying emotive meaning is 'laid bare'.

Let us give one more example of a formally heterogeneous monologue where a marked emotive climax is accompanied by a shift from RD into UDD:

79/ RŮŽENA: Maybe she'll learn something about Karel from that frog, maybe the frog will in his enthusiasm blab to Karel about her, Karel is jealous, Karel worries, Karel suffers terribly, Karel loves her again, Karel, Karel, how could you have done that to me, you don't know what love is. [PP]

This is part of a long interior monologue by Růžena who has just been repudiated by Karel; by its varied formal structure and masterly style, this monologue represents one of the highest achievements of modern Czech prose. It adequately expresses the dynamism of the innermost thoughts and feelings of a human being at a time of crisis. Here we can observe in minute detail how alternating devices of characters' speech work together with various other stylistic devices to achieve the final effect.

It can hardly be expected that every instance of the use of a particular device can be accounted for by semantic and/or emotive factors. There is good evidence for assuming that in many cases the choice of a device is determined primarily by purely formal considerations, such as the need for variation, the creation of a formal pattern, rhythm, etc. In one instance, especially, formal factors can be seen clearly at work: when the transition from DC to DN (or vice versa) is made smoother and more flexible by the use of UDD or RD.

At the beginning of this essay, the sequential structure of the traditional fictional text was described as a simple succession of portions of DN alternating with portions of DC equivalent to DD. Now, with the existence of a system of devices of characters' speech, this structure becomes much more complicated, allowing for transitions between various modes and with various 'degrees of smoothness'.[40] Here is an example to illustrate the point:

80/ [Beer] found both friends at Jasinko's. It was already growing dark and the rain made the room dim. Could Jasinko bring him about four wagonloads of timber? Why not? Tomorrow? All right. Then Abram Beer sat down on the bench in the corner. 'It's raining.' 'It's raining.' [ON]

The narrative goes into a portion of dialogue expressed in RD; a general tendency is sacrificed (question expressed in RD!) in favour of a smooth transition, materialized by RD sharing grammatical features of DN. Only then, after a short interruption by DN, the dialogue turns into its common form, DD.

The next example illustrates a similar situation, this time the transition from DN to interior monologue:

81/ Vašek observes him with fixed eyes, does not say a word. Daddy did not surprise him at all; he also gave that a thought. What should he reply to that? Nothing! We'll see; I'll think it over on the way. [OC]

Interior monologue very smoothly grows out of the narrative. RD provides a suitable transition, whereas UDD is chosen to express the outcome of the monologue.

Whatever semantic or emotive motivation could be found for splitting the dialogue (in example 80) and the interior monologue (in example 81) into two segments, the formal factor of 'smooth transition' could by itself account for this phenomenon.

I am convinced that it was the possibility of smooth transition which gave rise to one of the most typical and effective techniques in modern fiction, that of swift shifts from short portions of narrative to short portions of interior monologue, and vice versa. Two examples will demonstrate this well-known technique, the first using UDD, the second RD, to express the portions of interior monologue:

82/ At the next corner he [Prokop] stopped. / What now? There remains only

40 Formal definitions of the various 'degrees of smoothness' are suggested in my article 'Vers la stylistique structurale', *Travaux linguistique de Prague*, Prague, 1964, vol. I, p. 262f.

Carson. An unknown quantity who knows something and wants something. Good, Carson then. / Prokop found in his pocket the card which he had forgotten to mail and ran off to a post office. But at the mailbox his hand dropped. / Carson, Carson, yes, but he ... what he wants is hardly a trifle. ... Why is he looking for me? Evidently, Tomeš doesn't know everything. ... It must be something like that; but / (and here Prokop for the first time grew terrified at the extent to which he was involved) / is it possible, really, to reveal Krakatit? ... / Prokop began to get frightened of the whole business. / What devil is bringing that cursed Carson here? On all accounts it must be stopped, whatever the cost. [čk]

83/ The rhythm of his walk awoke memories which lined up one after another like his steps. / Did he actually have the green branch? ... Did he have such a gift? Yes, he had such a gift! / The answer made cold shivers run down Nikola's spine. The screaming of children died away long ago. / Perhaps he might actually have become Oleksa Dovbuš. Perhaps he had given up fame for a woman. ... / Nikola Šuhaj's pace became slower. The ground was spongy and his steps could not be heard any more. ... / How could he live so miserably and deplorably when he has a magic branch in his hand? [oN]

These two rather extensive examples are necessary for substantiating our interpretation of the technique. The shifts from narrative to interior monologue are facilitated because of the use of UDD and, especially, of RD; the reader gets an impression of the simultaneous unfolding of two fictional strata, that of the external world (in narrative) and of the internal world of a character (in interior monologue). A continuous and simultaneous confrontation of the 'stream-of-consciousness' of a character with the surrounding environment or accompanying actions is thus made possible. This is certainly one of the most dynamic techniques of modern psychological fiction. It contributes substantially to that general effect of dynamism and accelerated rhythm which, I feel, is one of the fundamental stylistic traits of modern fiction.

The present investigation of the functions of RD, its functional competition with DD and UDD, can only begin to outline general tendencies and indicate the variety of potential functions. We have ascertained that certain tendencies in the usage of the devices have developed; perhaps others are now developing. The general tendencies are conditioned primarily by the verbal features of the particular devices. Principally, however, the system of functions should be considered open, i.e., new functions, new ways of using the devices can be introduced in future works of fiction. Moreover, in the domain of functions, even more than in the domain of verbal form, a rather broad 'field of freedom' is given to the writer. Exercising this freedom, a writer can develop idiosyncratic modes in the usage of devices, 'deviating' from the general tendencies. Such 'deviations' will then contribute substantially to the formation of a writer's individual fictional style.

III DIFFUSED RD

Until now, we have supposed that RD, though grammatically identical with DN, can be clearly distinguished from sections of DN, representing a compact, delimited and well-defined portion of characters' speech (dialogue or interior monologue). In other words, we have accepted provisionally Bally's concept of RD as a device of pure reproduction, characterized by a 'strict distinction between the one who speaks or thinks, and the one who reports these utterances and thoughts'.[41] Let us designate this variant as *compact* RD.

However, the transitional character of RD, resulting from the presence of both the positive and the negative values of discriminative features in its verbal structure, makes the device 'unstable', and opens the possibility of substantial formal variation and functional shifts. Generally, the history of RD in modern fiction can be described as a process leading from the well-defined compact RD to the formation of a new variant of RD, ambiguous both in formal and functional respects.[42]

The ambiguous type of RD has already been discussed by M. Lips; she pointed out that in some novels, portions of text can be found which cannot be classified unequivocally as either narrative or characters' speech.[43] L. Spitzer, when analyzing a type of causal sentence in Charles-Louis Philippe's novel *Bubu de Montparnasse*, arrived at the conclusion that those sentences, though formally a part of the narrative, express thoughts 'in the terms of the acting characters, reasons which these characters refer to'.[44] He gave this device a special name – 'pseudoobjective discourse' – at the same time pointing to its kinship with RD. V.V. Vinogradov in his analysis of Tolstoy's *War and Peace* characterized the novel's narrative as a 'mass' where 'auctorial point of view, auctorial language alternates, blends

---

41 Ch. Bally, 'Figures de pensée et formes linguistiques', *GRM*, VI (1914), p. 421.
42 This ambiguous RD, arising against the background of a fully established RD, has to be distinguished from a not sufficiently marked RD which can be found in older fiction, representing the first stage of RD's development. A. Neubert called the latter 'auctorial RD'. (*Die Stilformen der 'erlebten Rede' im neueren englischen Roman*, Halle – Saale, 1957, p. 17f.)
43 Lips, *Style indirect libre*, pp. 57f., 101f.
44 L. Spitzer, Pseudoobjektive Motivierung bei Charles-Louis Philippe', *Stilstudien*, Munich, 1928, vol. II, p. 187.

and clashes with domains of characters' speech and thought'. He points to the intimate incorporation of interior monologue into narrative as the source of that device.[45]

The theoretical framework which we used for describing the compact variant of RD is also suitable for accounting for the ambiguous type; this fact proves the viability of the theory. It has been shown that formally (grammatically) RD is identical with DN. The formation of RD results in a concentration of positive discriminative features (deictic, allocutional, semantic, speech-level) on the formal base of DN. If the density of these features is sufficiently high, a compact and unambiguous form of RD arises. If the positive features are dispersed thinly, as sporadic signals on the DN base, the result is just a 'tinge' of DN; an ambiguous portion of text arises which blends positive signals with negative signals. In our frame of reference, this device could be called *diffused* RD. Because the formation of compact or diffused types of RD is a matter of the density, the concentration of the pertinent discriminative features, no rigid distinction between the two types can be made. They represent, rather, two opposite poles of the same phenomenon, with a broad transitional zone in between. In many cases, there is no possibility or need to decide explicitly what type of RD is present.

In the verbal structure of RD several prerequisites for its transformation into the diffuse variant can be pointed to:

First is the possibility of Czech RD developing a variant with past tense only, which leads to a full formal (grammatical) identification of RD with DN.

Second is the possibility of RD becoming integrated with a portion of DN in the framework of one sentence, one intonational unit; in such instances, the last 'demarcation line' between DN and RD has fallen down. Examples of this phenomenon are not extraordinarily frequent; nevertheless, from the theoretical point of view, they seem to be rather indicative:

84/ Director Vykoukal reviews his army with a general's eye, blue with anger, something is vexing him today, something private, / his son is enough to make a saint swear, it's nobody's business. [PP]

The loss of syntactic and intonational demarcation between DN and RD opens the road to the change of discriminative features into freely displaceable signals.

Thirdly, a semantic feature of DN may quite spontaneously penetrate into the verbal structure of RD. I am referring here to a designation of the speaker or hearer which is identical with his usual designation in DN; sometimes a personal pronoun is used together with the appositional name:

85/ JURAJ: Yes, *Juraj* came to *Nikola* and will stay with him. [ON]

86/ BRYCH: But he, *Brych*, cannot. [OC]

The explanation of this phenomenon lies in the fact that RD, with its reduction of grammatical persons, is unable to distinguish formally between speaker, hearer and the object of utterance. When such a distinction is needed, it has to be materialized by a direct naming of the speaker or hearer. Thus, a semantic feature of DN penetrates into the verbal structure of RD, blending with its DC features. This is, as already indicated, a spontaneous blending. When modern prose deliberately and systematically exploited the tensions inherent in the verbal structure of RD, the positive and negative discriminative features turned into 'liberated' signals with an infinite possibility of combinations, blending and mixing.

Diffused RD can be said to be DN penetrated and modified by a limited number of signals coming from DC. There is no need to undertake a thorough investigation of these signals; any of the positive features, discussed earlier, can be used as a signal of diffused RD. Some examples are given below.

Signals of *deixis*:

87/Again, Nikola looks at the lowlands. Down *over there* lies Koločava; a spread-out row of crumbs that could be swept together into a small pile and taken up in the palm of a hand. [ON]

Semantic signals – subjective attitude:

88/ Koločava is a *damned* village. A bit *like a Siberian settlement.* One lives here *as in occupied territory,* the people's looks are *surly* and, at the same time, *derisive.* [ON]

Semantic signals – subjective modality:

89/ Even the mother whose sons were sentenced to death broke bread and ate; she gets as hungry as anybody else, and, *perhaps*, gets overcome by fatigue and sleeps during the night; a person cannot stay awake a whole year; and, *perhaps,* even those imprisoned boys ... they also fall asleep sometimes and with what kind of dreams, *one wonders.* [PP]

Signals of specified speech level:

90/ When Helenka was finishing her *internship in orthopaedics,* there was in the *ward* a young man who had broken his thigh-bone. Such a *common femur fracture, a rather uninteresting case.* [PF]

With the development of diffused RD, the relationship between DN and DC changed dramatically. They are no longer compact and clearly demarcated planes, as they were in the traditional narrative text, but rather two opposite zones of maximal concentration of discriminative text features. In the broad transitional field, these discriminative features operate as independent signals, free to combine in contexts of various degrees of ambiguity. If the blend contains a high 'dose' of positive signals, a compact portion of RD on the base of DN can arise; in a lower degree of concentration, positive signals create an ambiguous portion of text, diffused RD, which could also be designated as *discourse* NC.

In modern prose, therefore, a dynamic relationship between DN and DC comes into existence, replacing their rigid separation (DN // DC) typical of the traditional narrative type. The following scheme is designed to give an approximative representation of the dynamic relationship:

$$\text{DN} \rightarrow \text{discourse NC (diffused RD)} \rightarrow \text{RD (compact RD)} \rightarrow \text{DC}$$

There are no well-defined boundaries in this dynamic relationship. On the contrary, a continuous field of transition exists between the pole of DN and that of DC. Ambiguity becomes a prominent and accepted quality of the fictional text. There are portions of text where we cannot decide whether it is DC penetrated by signals of DN, or DN tinged with signals of DC. These are simply mixed contexts where, as it were, both the narrator and a character 'speak' at the same time.

This explanation of the verbal status of discourse NC (diffused RD) enables us to describe and understand the function of the device in modern fiction. Diffused RD is not a device of 'reproduction', a verbal form for expressing dialogues or interior monologues of fictional characters. It is a specific narrative mode which is able to express a higher or lower degree of a character's involvement in the act of narration. A certain character (sometimes even several characters successively) takes over the primary functions of narrator, presenting, in the framework of the third-person form, a subjective point of view, a personal semantic aspect and attitude and sometimes even a highly idiosyncratic style. The fabric of narrative is interwoven with designs which express the individuality of a particular character. In the Introduction, I have suggested calling this mode of narrative *subjective Er-form.*

It is obvious that the traditional opposition of narrator and characters is abolished in the subjective narrative mode. The NC blend cannot be assigned to a homogeneous source; rather, a new totality of two combined sources of 'verbal behaviour', that of narrator and that of a character, is supposed to account for the verbal structure of discourse NC. It is a prime example of a 'double-voice expression' (*dvugolosoje slovo*),[46] the narrator's voice being inseparably fused with the voice of a character.

In detail, we can distinguish two distinct variants of the subjective narrative mode. In the first variant, a character's participation is suggested by semantic, deictic and other signals, but no speech-level shift from the norm of DN can be observed (example 91). In the second variant, a character's participation is expressed by all the possible positive signals, including the signals of a specified speech level; this results in a traceable speech-level shift in the narrative (example 92). The second variant of the subjective mode is the form of third-person narrative which comes closest to the first-person narrative (*Ich*-form), distinguished from it practically by grammatical form alone.

91/ *Maybe* they were still alive, those animals that Häusler and Růža ate raw. Ondřej would not put any in his mouth for all the world. But Růža who'd already *then*, on Christmas Eve in Nechleby, so bravely bitten into snails, encouraged by another *old gentleman, Uncle František,* was *now* gulping down oysters, that *disgusting slime which Ondřej could not even look at,* with the help of a drop of lemon, and wanted to flush it down with wine. [PP]

92/ Did not Dovbuša's cuirass emerge from the earth at Brazy? There, before his death, the famous robber of these mountains buried his flintlock rifle deep underground. And every year, the rifle moves a bit farther from the darkness to the earth's surface; and when the whole of it will glitter in the sun, like avens or anemone in the meadows in spring, the world will be given a new Oleksa Dovbuš, Dobvuš who took away from the rich and gave to the poor,

---

46 The term is suggested and explained by M.M. Bachtin in *Problemy tvorčestva Dostojevskogo* [Problems of Dostoyevsky's Art], Leningrad, 1929; see esp. the chapter 'Tipy prozaičeskogo slova' [Types of the Prosaic Word] reprinted in L. Matejka (ed.), *Readings in Russian Poetics*, Michigan Slavic Materials, 1962, vol. II, pp. 49–66.

beat the masters and never killed a soul except in just revenge or self-defence. [ON]

The viewpoint of Ondřej, the protagonist of Pujmanová's *People on the Crossroads* is very clearly expressed in example 91. At the same time, however, this portion of the narrative preserves the lexical variety and syntactic complexity which is generally characteristic of the style of narrative in Pujmanová's novel. In example 92, stylistic features of a folk myth are conspicuously present. Participation of a 'collective' character in narrative, the expression of 'voice of the people' through typical idioms of its myths, contributes to the overall characteristic of Olbracht's *Nikola Šuhaj, Robber* as a folk ballad.

Let us stress once more that the subjective narrative mode has substantially enriched the repertoire of narrative techniques in modern fiction and has become as widespread and as international as its closest relative, compact RD. Its expansion testifies again to the fact that modern literature, in various countries and under various ideologies, in its structural features and stylistic devices, represents a universal human phenomenon.

Analysis of RD and of its modification in modern fiction is a rather rewarding experience which contributes to a better understanding of some essential problems of the structural theory of literature. Although my investigation might seem to be guilty of a linguistic bias, I do not, as a matter of fact, believe in the sufficiency of a purely linguistic approach to literature. Literature is a totality of verbal and supraverbal levels designed to produce an aesthetic effect. Neglect of supraverbal structures and aesthetic effects makes some linguistic analyses of literature rather limited in their scope and validity. On the other hand, approaches to literature denying its verbal base are irrelevant for our understanding of literature as art.

An analysis of forms and functions (a 'means-ends model' in Jakobson's terminology)[47] demonstrates, in my opinion, the synthetic approach to literature. The investigation of RD confirms the general validity of the model. It has been shown that the aesthetic functions and effects of a literary device are determined by its verbal form. A thorough analysis of verbal forms is needed therefore in order to understand aesthetic effects. On the other hand, without analysing aesthetic functions and effects, we cannot expect to understand how the devices participate in the formation of the overall structure of a literary work of art.

47 R. Jakobson, 'Efforts toward a Means-End Model in Interwar Continental Linguistics' in *Trends in Modern Linguistics*, Utrecht, 1963, vol. II, pp. 104–8.

2
Composition of *The Labyrinth of the World and the Paradise of the Heart* by Jan A. Komenský (Comenius)

It is well known that the origins and first formulations of the structuralist theory of literature were parallel and closely linked to avant-garde experimental schools of literature and arts in the first decades of the twentieth century (such as futurism, cubism, poetism, surrealism, etc.).[1] It is therefore understandable that modern literature or experimental works of the eighteenth and nineteenth centuries became the favourite targets of structuralist investigation and interpretation. At the same time, however, earlier literature (especially medieval poetry), and folklore as well, were not excluded from the scope of the structuralists' interests. As a matter of fact, formal and structural analysis seems to be especially fascinating and rewarding when applied to the study of ancient and medieval literature; it is able to reveal the specific features characterizing 'old' literature as art and thus overcome the traditional approach which has treated older writings primarily as philological documents or ideological pronouncements.

Although formal and structural studies of 'old' literature have been much less frequent than those of modern, their contribution to our understanding of ancient and medieval literature as art is essential. With regard to medieval literature, these findings were summarized by Roman Jakobson

1 For a detailed account of the origins of the mutual relationship between modern poetry and modern poetics see: K. Pomorska, *Russian Formalist Theory and Its Poetic Ambiance*, The Hague – Paris, 1968. It has to be stressed, however, that an essential difference exists between the 'programmatic aesthetics of the avant-garde' and the 'theoretical aesthetics' of formalism and structuralism (cf. K. Chvatík, 'Mukařovského estetika a moderní umění' [Mukařovský's Aesthetics and Modern Art] in *Struktura a smysl literárního díla* [Structure and Meaning of the Literary Work], Prague, 1966, p. 41f.).

as follows: 'The literary art of the Middle Ages is so rich and varied, it is such a stupendous technical experience and, like the visual arts, it raised and solved so many problems of form ... that, in spite of some difficulties, our approach to this art can bring many fruitful stimuli to modern literary activity.'[2] And, taking into account the experience of recent decades, we can further claim that, without doubt, medieval, renaissance and baroque literature and art have been revived and have become part of our aesthetic experience and sensitivity.

The literary works of Jan A. Komenský (Comenius), 1592–1671, positively invite formal and structural analysis of their aesthetic forms, devices and qualities. Komenský is known primarily as an educationist, philosopher and political thinker;[3] but the form and style of his writings have been much praised and admired as well. Czech literary historians have repeatedly pointed out that Komenský employed a number of purely literary forms, used in medieval and renaissance literature, in order to convey his ideas to his readers in a more interesting and effective way.[4] This general observation holds true especially about Komenský's most popular work, the allegoric narrative *The Labyrinth of the World and the Paradise of the Heart* (first published in 1623).

Using the traditional theme of a pilgrimage through the World-City, *Labyrinth* distinguishes itself from numerous similar allegories in world literature and Czech literature by its artistic qualities and its elaborate style. It is precisely because of these aesthetic qualities that *Labyrinth* has outlived many now forgotten compositions of similar theme and genre.[5] In spite of its aesthetic qualities, intuitively perceived by both readers and

2 R. Jakobson, 'Dvě staročeské skladby o smrti' [Two Old Czech Compositions about Death], an introduction to the edition of *Spor duše s tělem* [Dispute between Soul and Flesh], Prague, 1927, p. 9.
3 Several books on Komenský's life and scholarly activity are available in English: J. Needham (ed.), *The Teacher of Nations*, Cambridge, 1942; M. Spinka, *John A. Comenius: That Incomparable Moravian*, Chicago, Ill., 1943; J. E. Sadler, *J. A. Comenius and the Concept of Universal Education*, London, 1966.
4 J. Heidenreich-Dolanský ascribed to some Komenský's works 'the character of drama' (*Český časopis filologický*, II (1943–4), p. 12). A. Škarka pointed to a group of Komenský's writings 'which borrowed their form and devices from belle-letters' (in his Afterword to a recent edition of *The Labyrinth of the World and the Paradise of the Heart*, Prague, 1958, p. 173). (Our quotations from the Czech original of *Labyrinth* refer to Škarka's edition.)
5 Without any doubt, *Labyrinth* has been the most popular work of 'old' Czech literature to this day. It has been translated into several languages. Two English translations are available, one by Count Lützow (New York, 1901), another by M. Spinka (Chicago, 1942); a revised edition of Spinka's translation has been published in the series Michigan Slavic Translations, no. 1, Ann Arbor, Mich., 1972.

literary historians, the formal structure of *Labyrinth* has not yet received sufficient attention from scholars. Aside from rather brief and superficial remarks about its form and style in general descriptions of Komenský's literary development, we can quote here only one investigation focused on the formal structure of *Labyrinth* – an essay by D. Čyževśkyj.[6] Čyževśkyj's analysis deserves attention because of its solid method and its revealing results; these results will be used in my investigation, although my focus of attention is different.

Even a perfunctory reading of *Labyrinth* conveys an impression of a harmonious balance of the parts and of a remarkable perfection of the whole. In my opinion, this impression is generated by the *symmetrical composition* of the work, and, therefore, the patterns of composition deserve special attention in the structural analysis of *Labyrinth*.

For the purposes of this essay, composition of a literary work will be conceived in a rather broad sense, as the organization of literary elements more complex than motifs. This means that composition is the organization of paragraphs, scenes, chapters, cycles of scenes and chapters, individual volumes in a more complicated structure (a trilogy, for example), etc. There is no need here to specify the notion of composition; however, a more elaborate and precise notional framework, differentiating various levels of composition, is one of the most topical tasks of the structural theory of literature.

The basic pattern of *Labyrinth*'s composition was pointed out by the author himself: The work consists of two contrasting parts, the first part depicting 'the Labyrinth of the World', the second, 'the Paradise of the Heart'.[7] Škarka, elaborating on this formulation, characterizes the two parts of *Labyrinth* as 'contrasts, antipoles,' and then goes on: 'The second part, the Paradise of the Heart, ... is like a mirror image of the first part. This is revealed immediately in its external composition, by the building up of the pilgrim's further destiny with a constant reference to the first

---

6 D. Čyževśkyj, 'Das Labyrinth der Welt und das Paradies des Herzens des J. A. Comenius', *Wiener Slavistisches Jahrbuch*, v (1956), pp. 59–85. Another investigation by Čyževśkyj is devoted to *Labyrinth's* themes and their sources (*Harvard Slavic Studies*, i (1953), pp. 83–135). Some observations on the formal features of *Labyrinth* can be found in J. Heidenreich-Dolanský's essay, quoted in footnote 4.

7 'The first part depicts figuratively the follies and vanities of the World, showing how mainly and with great labour it busies itself with worthless things, and how all these things at last end wretchedly, either in ridicule or in sorrow. The second part describes, partly allegorically, partly openly the true and firm felicity of the sons of God; how truly they are blessed who, turning their backs on the World and all worldly things, adhere to and indeed inhere in God.' (Dedication of *Labyrinth*, p. 9.)

part, to what he had already lived through; thus, Paradise of the Heart forms an almost symmetrical analogue to the first part.'[8]

Because 'Paradise of the Heart' is built up as an antinomy, a negation of the 'Labyrinth of the World', the relationship of the two parts could be called *negative symmetry*. Negative symmetry seems to be the basic principle of the composition of *The Labyrinth of the World and the Paradise of the Heart*. However, in contradistinction to the traditional view, I would like to argue that a *three-member*, rather than a two-member, symmetry can be revealed in the structure of *Labyrinth*. Three-member symmetry is a pattern consisting of two outer members symmetrical with a third, central member. Three-member positive symmetry can be represented by the formula A – B – A; three-member negative symmetry by A – B – Ā (non-A).[9]

The clue to the compositional pattern of *Labyrinth* can be found, in my opinion, by determining the narrative mode of the work and its modifications in the particular parts. The fundamental narrative mode in *Labyrinth* is a specific variant of the first-person narrative – the *rhetorical Ich-form*.[10] The rhetorical *Ich*-form is based on a consistent separation of the first-person narrator from the narrated events (actions). The narrator is a mere observer or witness of the depicted actions, characters and setting; he has no active role in the development of the action and does not belong to the gallery of acting characters. On the other hand, however (and this is the most prominent feature of the rhetorical *Ich*-form), the narrator is free to express his subjective interpretations of the narrated events in the form of commentaries or other evaluative devices. In other words, the narrator of the rhetorical *Ich*-form is not a detached reporter, but rather a partial interpreter.[11]

In the rhetorical *Ich*-form, the interpretative function of the narrator can be related sometimes to the ideological posture of the author himself. There is an 'ideological affinity' between the author and his narrator. This

---

8 Škarka, p. 186.

9 Whenever we speak about symmetry in literature, we have to bear in mind what Jakobson has pointed out with regard to parallelism (which, by the way, can be considered a specific type of two-member symmetry): 'Any form of parallelism is an apportionment of invariants and variables.' ('Grammatical Parallelism and its Russian Facet', *Language*, XLII (April-June, 1966), p. 423.) This means that any investigation of literary symmetry has to penetrate through the variable texture to reveal the underlying invariable structure.

10 In my essay 'The Typology of the Narrator: Point of View in Fiction' in *To Honour Roman Jakobson*, The Hague – Paris, 1967, vol. I, pp. 541–52, the mode was called *auctorial Ich*-form.

11 A detailed discussion of devices and effects of rhetoric in fiction is presented in the well-known monograph *The Rhetoric of Fiction* by Wayne C. Booth, Chicago, 1961.

affinity, however, has to be considered an extreme case in the scale of possible relationships between the author and the narrator (cf. Introduction, p. 13).

Taking the separation of the observing narrator and the observed, narrated action as a criterion, we can isolate three parts in the composition of *Labyrinth*. In the first part (chapters I – xxx), this antinomy is realized almost consistently throughout, with only a few 'deviations' which do not infringe upon the essence of the rhetorical type. In the second part (chapters xxxi – xxxv), this antinomy is modified in a specific manner, so that a transitional variant of the rhetorical *Ich*-form ensues. In the third part (chapters xxxvi – liv), the antinomy is practically void; a different mode of narrative (the personal *Ich*-form) emerges, with the distintegrated rhetorical mode leaving some formal residua in the text.

PART I OF *Labyrinth*

In the first part of *Labyrinth*, the separation of the narrator-observer and the observed narrated events is implemented in the antinomy between the pilgrim and his two companions (on the one hand) and the World (on the other). The World can be said to consist of depicted characters, their actions and setting. The pilgrim-narrator is not an acting character; he is not involved in motifs and episodes of the World (with some exceptions which we will touch upon briefly later on). The same holds true about the pilgrim's companions ('interpreters'), Ubiquitous and Delusion. The distinction of the *observers' plane* (pilgrim and his companions) and the *narrated plane* (the World) will be called the primary opposition in the composition of part I of *Labyrinth*. Moreover, in the observers' plane, there exists a secondary opposition, that between the pilgrim-narrator and his companions. Whereas the primary opposition is expressed mainly in narrative, the secondary opposition finds its expression in the form of dialogue.

For the purpose of this study there is no need to go into a detailed analysis of the narrated plane. It seems to be treated as one, compact compositional element. Let us, however, note one rather important stylistic feature of the narrated plane, one already analysed by Čyževśkyj: expressions of motifs of the narrated plane are very often clustered in chains of various length (and various semantic character).[12] Čyževśkyj gives a detailed account of these chains; here, let us quote just one example:

---

12 Čyževśkyj did not attribute this stylistic feature to the narrated plane only; rather, he considered it a general quality of Komenský's 'baroque' style.

1/ Some, indeed, collected refuse and divided it amongst themselves; some rolled timber and stones to and fro or hoisted them up by pulleys, and then let them down again; some dug up earth and conveyed or carried it from place to place; the rest occupied themselves with little bells, mirrors, bellows, rattles, and other trinkets; some played even with their own shadows, measuring, chasing, catching them. And all this so vigorously that many groaned and sweated, and some even injured themselves.

The grouping of expressions in chains is an outstanding peculiarity of the texture of the narrated plane in *Labyrinth*; as we shall show in detail, there is no clustering of expressions in chains in the observers' plane.[13]

It was proposed in the Introduction (p. 8) to characterize the rhetorical *Ich*-narrator by a combination of the representational and the interpretative functions. In part I of *Labyrinth*, the two functions are expressed consistently and explicitly:

1 The representational function assumes the specific form of observation. Introductory phrases, presenting the motifs of the World as the narrator's observations and perceptions, are the basic device of this function; verbs like *see, look, catch sight of, behold, hear*, etc. (*vidět, hledět, spatřit, pozorovat, slyšet*, etc.) are typical of these phrases. These verbs are limited in their types,[14] are highly repetitive and do not form chains. Let us quote here one of the many instances of 'observation description' which represents an important component of part I of *Labyrinth*:

2/ We then entered the street, and behold, there was a host of people all in couples, but many, as it seemed to me, most unequally joined, large with small, handsome with ugly, young with old, and so forth. And watching carefully what they were doing, and in what the sweetness of this state consisted, I saw that they looked at each other, spoke to one another, and sometimes even caressed or kissed one another.

13 The distinguishing feature can be used also as a formal criterion for assigning a structural element to one of the compositional planes. Thus, for example, Death belongs to the narrated plane, because the expressions of its motifs are clustered in chains: 'Some he (Death) merely wounded, lamed, blinded, deafened, or stunned.' (*Labyrinth*, p. 28.)

14 'Type' is used here in the sense of lexical statistics, designating lexical units (*lexemes*) characterized by the unity of lexical meaning; occurrences are various forms of the type to be found in texts. Thus, for example, 'see' is type with occurrences such as 'I see', 'he saw', 'she did not see', etc.

2 The interpretative function constantly accompanies the representational function. Consistently and from a fixed point of view, the narrator pronounces his attitudes and value judgements. Many motifs of the World are tinted with subjective semantic and/or emotive contextual components:

3/ I also perceived other disorder, blindness and folly.

Since the subjective component is superimposed on the motifs of the narrated plane, chain formation is not unexpected here. On the other hand, when a direct expression of the narrator's attitude is incorporated into the narrative, chains cannot be found. This holds true about such common verbs of emotive or ideological attitude as: *to have a liking for, to fall into disfavour, to marvel at, to be horrified, to become frightened,* etc. (*líbit se, znelíbit se, divit se, zděsit se, uleknout se,* etc.).

A quite frequent device of the narrator's interpretative function is his interior monologue. This device is especially suited to the rhetorical *Ich*-form: it enables the narrator to express a 'silent' commentary without trespassing the barrier between the narrator and the depicted characters (as would happen in the case of an uttered value judgement). In interior monologue, the narrator's evaluation is addressed to himself (and 'overheard' by the reader); no verbal contact with the characters of the narrated plane is established:

4/ I merely thought to myself: 'This is indeed a wondrous government of the World. The king is a woman, the councillors are women, the officials are women; the whole rule is of women. How could anyone fear it?'

It is very interesting to find that, in many instances, the narrator's rhetoric follows a pattern of negative symmetry: the narrator's first impressions are positive; after a more thorough examination, however, the narrator hands down a final negative judgement. Let us, for example, follow the shift in narrator's rhetoric regarding the society of so-called 'Rosicrucians':

5/ Hearing such words I myself began to rejoice, and to feel hopes that, God willing, I also should receive somewhat of that upon which others were counting. ... Consequently, some were in despair, while others, looking round and seeking new roads to find these men, were again disappointed, until I myself was grieved, seeing no end to this. ... 'Is nothing, then, to come of all this? Alas, my hopes!'

Sometimes, the reversal of a value judgement is rather sudden, without any motivation, as in the case concerning *juris prudentia*:

6/ Then I said: 'This is a fine thing!' Yet after watching it awhile, the matter grew disgusting to me.

In the narrator's consistent rhetoric, in his recurrent value judgements and commentaries, a rounded-off ideological and ethical attitude towards the World is expressed. In the first part of *Labyrinth*, this attitude is almost entirely negative or negative, at least, in its final purport (after the initial positive evaluation has been dismissed as superficial). It should not surprise us that a positive counterpart to this negative attitude is to be found in part III of the work; here, the narrator finds a World that measures up to his ideals and is in full accord with his ideology; now his rhetoric can pour forth enthusiasm and praise. Symptomatically enough, positive value judgements in part I occur only in instances where the narrated event anticipates an event of the ideal World (cf., for example, the positive reaction to a statement by Paul of Tarsus, chapter XI).

The general typology of narrative mode denies any action function to the rhetorical *Ich*-narrator. We have to bear in mind, however, that the rhetorical *Ich*-form, while keeping the narrator consistently outside the narrated plane, needs a set of motifs to bring the observing narrator into contact with the represented actions. A *narrator's situation*, strictly separated from the narrated action, is typical for the observing *Ich*-narrator; it is expressed by a set of motifs which will be called narrator's motifs (N-motifs).

In part I of *Labyrinth*, the narrator's situation can be summarized as a pilgrimage through the allegorical World-City. The motifs of the pilgrimage are concentrated mainly in chapters I to IV, where the motivation of the pilgrimage, the meeting with companions, the 'transfer of magic gifts',[15] and the ascent up the observation tower are depicted. While in chapters I to IV, N-motifs dominate the narrative, in the following chapters they form a subordinated, though continuous action-line expressing the pilgrim's wandering through the City along particular streets and quarters.

Various verbs of 'passing' and 'changing place' characterize the N-motifs, verbs such as: *descend, approach, squeeze through, come, enter,* etc. (*zejít, přistoupit, protlačit se, přijít, vejít,* etc.); or *they are leading me, they would place me on,* etc. (*vedou mne, postaví mne na,* etc.). For the

15 Cf. V. Propp, *Morfologija skazki* [Morphology of the Folk-tale], Leningrad, 1928; English translation (ed. by S. Pirkova-Jakobson), Bloomington, Indiana, 1958, pp. 14, 40.

structure of *Labyrinth* one fact is of utmost importance: these expressions are limited in their 'types'; they have a high repetition and never are grouped in chains.

Simplicity and repetitiveness of texture has been observed with all the motifs assigned to the narrator (observational, rhetorical, action motifs). This texture produces an effect of stylistic monotony and sobriety of the narrator's plane which is in crass contrast to the rich, ornate, 'baroque' style of the narrated plane. The stylistic contrast between the two planes reflects the governing principle of negative symmetry which controls every aspect of the structure of *Labyrinth*.

It has been pointed out in the Introduction that the narrator's participation in the narrated action draws the line between the rhetorical and the personal *Ich*-form. This means that a deviation from the norm of the rhetorical *Ich*-form arises whenever the pilgrim-narrator gives up his role of mere observer and becomes involved in the action of the narrated World. The most important instances of the narrator's transgression into the World are the episodes of his marriage (chapter viii), of the storm at sea (chapter ix) and of his priesthood (chapter xviii).

It is well known from existing literature that all these episodes are autobiographical in character. The author's biography is their common source, and only from this viewpoint do they seem to be coherent. Within the narrated action, the episodes are purely accidental, interpolated without being integrated in the chain of narrated events and without forming a coherent action-line. They emerge wherever narrated events recall events of the author's biography. This association is their only link with the narrated plane. Otherwise they remain episodic fragments, without motivation or consequences in the concatenation of motifs of the narrated action. This accidental and fragmentary character is also typical of all the other, less important episodes and motifs of the narrator's participation in the narrated plane.

This negative statement can certainly account for our treating these episodes and motifs as deviations from the norms of the rhetorical mode rather than as indicators of a shift in narrative mode. At the same time, however, we can suggest that they also do fulfill a certain positive function. As mentioned earlier, the rhetorical *Ich*-form sometimes reveals an ideological affinity between the narrator and the author. It seems to me that the episodes of the narrator's participation in the narrated action, being so conspicuously autobiographical, contribute toward creating an impression of this affinity. Motifs of the narrator's situation, because of their purely fictitious and allegorical nature (pilgrimage through the World-City, magic gifts, strange companions), bring about a rather strict separation of the 'fictitious' narrator from the 'real' author. Autobiographical motifs, which are realistic in the strict sense, are needed to bridge the distance between the allegorical pilgrim and the real, contemplating author.

The narrator's attempts to communicate with the characters of the World represent another set of 'deviations' from the norms of the rhetorical *Ich*-form. Characteristically, in part I of *Labyrinth*, the narrator fails in all these attempts. In every instance, he is immediately and quite rudely repudiated, and the barrier between the narrator and the characters of the World is promptly re-erected. In other words, these attempts at verbal contact – similar to the narrator's participation in the actions of the World – are no more than occasional fragments.

After all, even if we could not find a reasonable interpretation for every deviation from the norms of the rhetorical *Ich*-form, our specification of the narrative mode in part I of *Labyrinth* would not be invalidated. Narrative mode (as any abstract literary category) is of typological nature and, therefore, its norms are not expected to be perfectly realized in the particular manifestations of the mode. (Cf. here, p 17.) Our identification of the narrative mode in part I of *Labyrinth* is based on fundamental properties and predominant features of the text.

Non-involvement in the narrated plane, in the actions and episodes of the World, is a common property of both elements of the observer's plane – the pilgrim-narrator and his two companions. At the same time, both the pilgrim-narrator and his companions are related to the narrated World through their interpretative function. Finally, in part I of *Labyrinth*, the companions are the pilgrim's partners in unfolding the sequence of N-motifs which we called the narrator's situation: they invite the pilgrim to wander through the World-City, they provide him with 'magic gifts' and they accompany him on his pilgrimage.

However, with these general functions, the structural affinity of the pilgrim and his companions is exhausted. A fundamental difference dominates their relationship: they represent an antinomy of semantic and emotive attitudes, resulting from two contradictory systems of values – one system negating the World, the other defending it. The secondary opposition in the composition of *Labyrinth* results from this semantic and emotive antinomy, manifesting itself in a special form of semantically 'tense' dialogue, in *dispute*.

There is a tradition of dispute in medieval Czech literature; it is important for our study that the pattern of a medieval dispute is designated as 'negative parallelism'.[16] Negative parallelism, of course, readily integrates with the general principle of negative symmetry governing the composition of *Labyrinth*. The dialogue between the the pilgrim and his

16 Jakobson, p. 23, see footnote 2.

companions is truly a dialogue with 'an *a priori* known result' (Jakobson) or with no result at all. It is a verbal form of an unsolvable conflict between two opposing ideologies; usually, it is rather abruptly ended by one of the partners, as if this partner had become aware of the absurdity of any dialogue between two rigid, 'closed' systems of values. The dialogue is a purely verbal conflict, without any attempt to understand the partner's attitude, even without any genuine argumentation. There is no solution to the conflict; yet, the conflict crops up again and again, incited by some event in the narrated World.[17] The event evokes, as a rule, a negative value judgement on the part of the pilgrim, whereas his companions' reactions are always positive. Clashes between negative and positive rhetoric are so frequent that only a brief example is necessary for illustration:

7/ Seeing this, I said: 'What a folly, to wish to make mere followers and flatterers of their leaders and advisers!' 'That is the way of the World,' said the interpreter, 'and it does not do any harm. If those whiners were given entire freedom, who knows what they would not dare to do ...'

It has to be pointed out, however, that the *rhetorical dispute* – expressing the secondary opposition in the structure of *Labyrinth* – is only one of two principal types of dialogue in *Labyrinth*. Another perhaps not less important type is the *informative dialogue* expressing motifs of the observed World. This type differs from the rhetorical dispute both in its form and in its semantics.[18] Usually, it consists of a brief question (pilgrim) and a descriptive answer (companions); it has a low semantic tension, easily passing into a short monologue expressed by one of the 'interpreters'. The companions' answers, giving description and explanation of the events of the narrated World, evidently fulfill the same function as observation descriptions in the narrative:

8/ 'What will it be?' quoth I. He answered: 'The academy will now crown those who, having been more diligent than the others, have reached the summit of arts.'

17 The conflict between the narrator and his companions comes to its peak in chapter xxviii (a quarrel) and in chapter xxx where the pilgrim is indicted by his companions. But even here, when the conflict ceases to be purely verbal, no solution is given; no trial is ever held.

18 Our discussion of the semantics of dialogue is based on a fundamental investigation into these rather neglected problems done by J. Mukařovský in his essay 'Dialog a monolog' [Dialogue and Monologue] in *Kapitoly z české poetiky* [Chapters from Czech Poetics], Prague, 1948, vol. i, pp. 129–53.

Understandably enough, in many instances it is difficult to decide whether a dialogue is rhetorical or informative; moreover, we find text portions where one type passes over into the other one:

9/ And I asked: 'Who are these men, and what are they doing?' My interpreter answered: 'They are the most subtle philosophers, who accomplish that which the heavenly sun, with its heat, cannot in many years effect in the bowels of the earth; that is, to raise divers metals to their highest degree – to gold.' 'But wherefore is this?' I said; 'for surely iron and other metal are of greater use than gold?' 'What a dolt thou art!' he said; 'for gold is the most precious thing; he who has it fears not poverty.'

Observation description and informative dialogue are two structural elements, integrating motifs of the narrated plane (characters, actions and setting of the World) into the overall compositional pattern. On the other hand, the narrator's value judgements and dispute are two elements of interpretation. The last structural element of the observers' plane, the set of N-motifs, is relevant only as a prerequisite for materializing the specific compositional pattern of Komenský's work.

The results of this analysis can be summarized in the following conclusion: The composition of part I of *Labyrinth* results from the principle of negative symmetry operating on a rather limited set of structural elements. The principle determines the combination and the mutual relationships of these elements (see Scheme 1, p. 77). Anticipating the results of further analysis, we can state that, in parts II and III of *Labyrinth*, no new structural elements will enter the picture. Only new combinations and some modifications within the closed system will account for the compositional changes occurring in these parts.

PART II OF *Labyrinth*

The second part of *Labyrinth*, representing the central member of the negative symmetry, tells the story of Solomon and his company (chapters XXXI – XXXV).[19] As far as the narrative mode is concerned, this part is some-

---

19 For the structural theory of literature it would be most interesting to discuss the consequences of text changes (variants) for the interpretation of a literary structure. It is known that the Solomon episode was added to the 1631 edition of *Labyrinth*. We have to assume that only then the original two-member negative symmetry was transformed into a three-member one.

thing of a transition between parts I and III: On the surface, the mode remains the same as in part I; it is rhetorical *Ich*-form; the pilgrim-narrator continues to be a witness and commentator of Solomon's rise and fall. At the same time, a new narrative mode is initiated or, at least, intimated in part II – the *personal Ich-form*. This narrative mode will become predominant in part III.

As we know, the narrator of the personal *Ich*-form is assigned all primary and secondary functions: representational (coupled with the controlling function), interpretative and action functions. The barrier between the narrator and the narrated action does not exist in this narrative mode.

In part II of *Labyrinth*, a specific incipient variant of the personal *Ich*-form can be disclosed. The functions of the personal *Ich*-narrator are assigned to two different, but closely related subjects: the representational and interpretative functions continue to be fulfilled by the pilgrim, whereas the action function is assigned to Solomon (and, later, to his companions).

Our interpretation is based on the assumption that from the functional point of view (i.e. with regard to their role in the composition), the pilgrim and Solomon are fungible elements. In other words, we suppose that there exists a close functional affinity between the pilgrim and Solomon such that Solomon can be considered a symbolic deputy of the pilgrim in the narrated plane. Solomon's role is to attempt a reform of the World 'within' the World. The tragic end of Solomon's attempt demonstrates once and for all the futility of reform efforts and brings about the final argument for a complete rejection of the World and for the necessity of retiring into the 'Paradise of the Heart'. It appears likely that Solomon's reformative enthusiasm and failure were meant to symbolize Komenský's own pan-reformatory endeavours and their futility. In other words, the link between Solomon and the narrator can be extended to the author himself. The affinities binding Solomon, the pilgrim-narrator and author Komenský together are the skeleton of the complex symbolic and allegorical network in part II of *Labyrinth*.

In this context, we are interested only in the affinities between the pilgrim-narrator and Solomon; these are evidenced in several structural features of the work:

1 An obvious similarity exists between the pilgrim's variance with the Queen of the World and Solomon's revolt against her. The chain of motifs indicating this affinity is initiated as early as chapter XXX where the pilgrim is indicted before the Queen. However, this episode remains a fragment and the pilgrim again retreats into his observer's background; in-

stead, Solomon (and later his companions) replaces the pilgrim as the Queen's antagonist.

2 Before entering the narrated action as an acting character, Solomon temporarily performs the function of an observer (chapter xxxii). But after accumulating some experience about the World, he expresses, in the same vein as the pilgrim has, his retorical condemnation of its order. His rhetoric leads to action, to a revolt against the Queen of the World. In this way, the pilgrim and Solomon, as it were, exchange roles: the pilgrim, who was about to become an acting character in open conflict with the Queen, retreats to his observation post; Solomon, who was for some time accumulating information about the World as an observer, turns into an active protagonist in the episode of revolt. The common background which makes this exchange of roles possible is the negative attitude towards the World expressed in both the pilgrim's and Solomon's rhetoric.

3 The manifestation of both the pilgrim's and Solomon's negative attitude towards the World is *mudrování*, i.e. original, unconventional cogitation about the World and its values (in English translations this is rendered by various expressions such as 'carping', 'cavilling', 'playing a wiseacre', 'sophistry', etc.). It is very interesting to follow the wandering of the motif of *mudrování* (which we translate uniformly as 'carping') through the structure of *Labyrinth*; it becomes a kind of leitmotif, linking together all the representatives of the opposition against the World.

In part i, this motif is rather often found in the companions' utterances, with a warning tone addressed to the pilgrim:

10/ 'Thou wilt not cease thy carping ... till thou hast come to harm.'

'Indeed, I promise thee that if thou ceasest not to carp thou shalt find thyself in a place that will please thee not.'

'Now, do not carp so much ... believe others rather than thyself.'

At the end of part i, the motif passes into a speech of the Queen of the World, again addressed to the pilgrim with reproach:

11/ 'But this I hear of thee with displeasure, that thou art somewhat fastidious; and though thou should learn in the World as a new guest, yet thou givest thyself up to carping.'

Characterized by the same warning tone, the motif of *mudrování* then reappears in an utterance of the assistants to the Queen; however, this time the addressees are Solomon's companions:

12/ Since the wisest of men, Solomon, had submitted his mind, and become accustomed to the ways of the World, as all might see, why should they walk apart from the others and continue to carp?

Here, the motif expresses the coupling of the narrator-pilgrim with Solomon's group. This coupling is then reinforced by a generalized statement made by one of the pilgrim's companions; *mudrování* is explicitly designated as being the reason for the cruel punishment of Solomon's companions; addressed again to the pilgrim, it conveys a clear warning to him:

13/ 'Now wilt thou learn what happens to those who, by their carping, stir up riots and storms in the World.'

It seems to me that these examples are sufficient evidence of the compositional links between the pilgrim and Solomon's group expressed by the leitmotif of *mudrování*.

4 Immediately after Solomon has taken a stand against the World, the pilgrim associates himself with the new hero and expresses his empathy with positive rhetoric [248]. As we already know, positive rhetoric is rather rare before part III of *Labyrinth*, and, if expressed, it is usually very soon dismissed. It is interesting to note that no additional negative commentary about Solomon is made, though he did not fulfil the pilgrim's hopes. Nevertheless, the basic pattern of positive and negative rhetoric is preserved in this case as well; however, the negative judgement is not inflicted upon Solomon, but rather as a final condemnation upon the World which has failed to respond to Solomon's reform efforts and, instead, has corrupted him. After the disaster which befalls Solomon's companions, the pilgrim-narrator gives up his last hope for a better World order:

14/ I see now that matters will not become better in the World. All my hopes are ended. Woe on me!

This is the final commentary of Solomon's episode; it gives the motivation for the fundamental shift in the action and composition of *Labyrinth* – for the escape from the World into the privacy of the Heart.

The links between the pilgrim and Solomon (Solomon's group) confirm our basic assumption about the functional affinity of the two structural elements. Solomon is a symbolic deputy of the pilgrim in the episode of the revolt against the World and its 'ways'. At the same time, however, formal differentiation of the two structural elements makes it possible to distinguish the second part of *Labyrinth* from the third one. Whereas in part III the pilgrim himself enters the narrated plane, in part II the functional substitution just described makes it possible to preserve a fundamental separation of the narrator from the narrated plane. The pilgrim remains a non-acting, commenting observer and narrator of the episode; at the same time, a functional substitute is delegated to the narrated plane to participate actively in the development of the narrated action.

If we accept this interpretation of Solomon and of his role, then we can repeat our earlier statement that no new structural elements appear in the composition of part II. Solomon is a functional 'double' of the narrator-pilgrim and his negative attitude towards the narrated World is equivalent to the antinomy 'pilgrim – World'.

PART III OF *Labyrinth*

The third part of *Labyrinth* is essentially different from the preceding two parts, with respect both to its composition and to its style. Nevertheless, a closer analysis reveals that the relationship between parts I and II, on the one hand, and part III, on the other, cannot be described as a contradiction only; an underlying structural kinship of all three parts of *Labyrinth* also exists. As already indicated, this general similarity is based on the identity of the basic structural elements which combine to set up the composition of the three parts: the observation description, the rhetorical commentary and the dialogue-dispute. The specificity of part III arises from the fact that combinations, mutual relationships and hierarchy of the three basic elements are here essentially different from those in parts I and II.

These transformations are a direct consequence of a basic change in the relationship of the observers' and the narrated planes. As we know, this antinomy is impaired, in a specific way, already in part II; now, in part III, it is practically abolished by two essential changes: first, the disappearance of the pilgrim's companions; second, the narrator's taking over the role of an acting character. However, some residua of the observation structure will be found in part III, hinting at the disintegrated narrative mode of the rhetorical *Ich*-form. In this respect, the observation residua can be said to have a significance similar to the episodes of the narrator's 'epic' activity in part I which anticipate the narrative mode of part III: they indicate the underlying structural unity of the whole work.

Perhaps the relationship of the two functions of the pilgrim-narrator can best be described in terms of the 'dominant':[20] Whereas in the first and second parts, the function of observation dominates and the activity in the narrated events is suppressed, in the third part, the hierarchy of the two functions is reversed. At the same time, all three parts are united by the narrator's interpretative function which, in parts I and II, is predominantly negative (with respect to the narrated World), and in part III, predominantly positive.

A simple schematic representation could perhaps contribute to a better understanding of the shifts in the hierarchy of the narrator's functions and of the ensuing transformation of the narrative type:

Table 1

	I	II	III
Narrator's Functions a) observation b) action	*pilgrim* *pilgrim*	*pilgrim* *Solomon*	*pilgrim* *pilgrim*
Type of *Ich*-form	*rhetorical* (with traces of personal)	*rhetorical* (with a symbolic personal)	*personal* (with residua of rhetorical)

Part III of *Labyrinth* is introduced by a transition consisting of chapters XXXVI – XXXVII. After the conclusion of the Solomon episode, these chapters return briefly to the narrative mode of part I – the observation descriptions of the dying and dead and of the 'chamber of the Heart'. However, as early as chapter XXXVIII the new compositional pattern is introduced by the pilgrim's receiving a new companion – Christ. By the introduction of Christ as the pilgrim's new companion and partner, a fundamental transformation of one basic structural element – the dialogue – is accomplished: it is no longer a dispute, a dialogue of conflict, but a friendly dialogue with no semantic tension, one easily passing into a monologue delivered by Christ.

A dialogue between the pilgrim and Christ represents the first portion of part III. With this, a characteristic device of part III is introduced: negative parallelism with respect to the first part. Christ is a contrary substitute for the pilgrim's previous companions. However, the accent in the

20 The notion of 'dominant' was introduced into the structural theory of literature by J. Tynjanov in his *Problema stichotvornogo jazyka* [The Problem of Verse Language], Leningrad, 1924; later on, it was elaborated by R. Jakobson and J. Mukařovský.

negative parallelism is on the World: Christ's monologue, in its particular paragraphs, summarizes the pilgrim's experience from his observing the World and consistently negates the motifs of the World with the motifs of 'eternal bliss in Christ':

15/ 'Thou hast seen in the second estate how the men who seek gain busy themselves with endless labours, what artifices they employ, what perils they risk. Thou must consider all this striving as vanity, knowing that one thing alone is necessary, the favour of God. Therefore, limiting thyself to the one calling which I have entrusted to thee, conduct thy labours faithfully, conscientiously, quietly, leaving to me the end and aim of all things.'

'Those others find their joy in plentiful banquets, eating, drinking, laughter. Let thy delight be, when necessary, to hunger, thirst, cry, suffer blows and all other afflictions, for my sake and with me.'

From the predominantly dialogic first portion, part III of *Labyrinth* moves to its second phase which is focused on the narrator's description of the 'World of True Christians'. There are, however, fundamental differences between this narrative and the narrative of part I. First of all, there is little left of the narrator's situation, of the description of the pilgrimage. Only isolated N-motifs are interspersed in the narrative, such as: *when I came nearer, when I had proceeded farther, now when I had walked sufficiently among these Christians.* We can say that N-motifs are no more than disconnected fragments, surviving only as stylistic stereotypes. A coherent description of the narrator's situation is no longer necessary, because the narrator's situation converges with the narrated action.

There is also little left of the observation function of the narrator. As with the N-motifs, observation expressions are no more than formal introductions, used only because of habit (*I saw, I found, I have heard*). Observation descriptions, introduced by such expressions, are replaced or, at least, combined with unmediated descriptions (i.e. descriptions with no introductory phrases). A typical passage of the text shall demonstrate the 'mixed' character of the narrative in the second portion of part III:

16/ Verily, God had deprived these men of stony hearts and placed in their bodies hearts of flesh, pliant and yielding to His will. And although the devil, with his crafty suggestions, the World, with its corrupting examples, the flesh, with its natural reluctance in the good, troubled them much, yet they cared not for any of these things, driving the devil away by the artillery of their prayers, guarding themselves against the World by the shield of resolute will and compelling their bodies to obedience by the scourge of discipline. ... I saw not that anyone among them claimed absolution from his sins because of the weakness of the flesh, or excused his evil deeds by the frailness of human nature. Rather did I see that if a man had surrendered his whole heart to Him who had created it, redeemed it, and sanctified it for His temple, then following his heart, his other limbs also freely and gradually took that direction to which God willed them. Oh, Christian, whoever thou art, free thyself from the fetters of flesh, examine, try and learn that the obstacles which thou imaginest in thy mind are far too small that they could impede thy will, if it is sincere.

The passage starts with an unmediated description, only later turning into a description formally introduced by observation expressions (*I saw, did I see*). It is concluded by a rhetorical apostrophe addressed to the reader and based on the narrator's own conviction. This appeal indicates a shift in narrator's rhetoric; in part III, this rhetoric becomes rather a means of personal confession, very often addressed to the reader.

While the emergence of unmediated descriptions is the most evident consequence of the change in the narrative technique, the increase of motifs of narrator's participation in the narrated events in the second portion of part III is lower than expected. This is due to a general limitation of action in part III. Nevertheless, it is quite obvious that the relationship between the narrator and the narrated World has changed: the narrator freely communicates with the characters, associates himself with their actions, gets benediction from their priest, and finally, participates in the homage to the Lord amid the crowd of Saints and true Christians (chapter LII). Here, the role of the narrator, as an observer, comes to its final end.

An association of the pilgrim-narrator with the narrated plane is explicitly expressed in an interesting stylistic device appearing in chapter XLVIII: first in the form of a spontaneous 'reported' speech, then even without this motivation, the first person plural is used to express a judgement about the principles and orders of the True Christians:

17/ They also said that the World showed no indulgence likewise toward its own; indeed, it scratches, deceives, robs, torments them; let it then do the same to us; who cares? If we cannot escape the torment, we will endure it so that the losses inflicted upon us by the World may be recompensed by the bountiful goodness of God. Thus their derision, hatred and injury shall be turned to our profit.

Why should a Christian torment himself over it, if his conscience is righteous and he has the grace of God in his heart? If men will not conform to our customs, let us then conform to theirs as far as our conscience permits. The World, it is true, is going from bad to worse, but will our fretting improve it?

The first person plural, quite unthinkable in parts I and II, indicates the degree of integration of the narrator into the narrated World.[21] This is also one of the devices which, together with other common devices (exclamations, allocutions, adorations, etc.), makes the rhetoric of part III a kind of personal confession. Moreover, taking into account a general reduction of action, we can understand why part III produces quite a specific stylistic effect: in contrast to the more 'fictional' ('epic') parts I and II, part III reads like a tract.

The second portion of part III continues to build up the pattern of negative parallelism with respect to part I. Chapters L and LI, on the whole, are based on this principle. Not only the arrangement of motifs, but even the syntactic structure and the selection of vocabulary are determined by the pattern of negative parallelism:[22]

18/ I saw here that everything was contrary to the ways of the World. In the World I beheld everywhere blindness and darkness, here clear light; in the World deceit, here truth; in the World everything was full of disorders, here there was the purest order; in the World tumult, here peace; in the World care and anxiety, here joy; in the World want, here abundance; in the World slavery and bondage, here freedom ...

As I had previously observed in the World much unquietude and toil, anxiety and care, horror and fear among all estates, so I now found here much peace of mind and good cheer in all those who had surrendered themselves to God.

Instead of those steely fetters, I saw here golden clasps; instead of endeavours to separate, I saw joyful union both of bodies and of hearts.

The second portion of part III is not, however, the finale of *Labyrinth*. A short third portion (chapters LIII and LIV) iterates the structure of the

---

21 The coalescence of observation with the narrator's interior experience can be documented also by the following stylistic detail: *I saw, I saw, I saw and learned* that to have within you God, with His celestial treasures, is so glorious a thing ... (*Labyrinth*, p. 157.)

22 Here we can also refer to Čyževśkyj's distinction of word chains of the 'first' and the 'second' group (*Wiener Slavistisches Jahrbuch*, v (1956), p. 81).

first portion; again, it is a dialogue between the pilgrim and Christ, this time leading to the pilgrim's closing monologue expressing his prayer of thanks. Thus, a secondary pattern of positive three-member symmetry can be discovered in the composition of part III: Pilgrim – Christ dialogue; World of True Christians; Pilgrim – Christ dialogue. This symmetry, of course, is integrated into the framework of the primary negative symmetry of parts I – II – III. This confirms not only our assumption about symmetry (combined with parallelism) as the fundamental compositional pattern of *Labyrinth*; it indicates also the intricacy of the interwoven symmetric patterns which, on several levels of composition, govern the combinatorics of structural elements, creating the final harmony of the whole.

A simplified representation of the composition of *Labyrinth*, given in Scheme I following, indicates the intricacy of its symmetric structure. The scheme once again confirms the assertion that the whole complex structure of *Labyrinth* is made up of a rather limited number of fundamental elements linked by positive (+) or negative (−) relationships. Governed by the principle of symmetry, these elements and relationships combine into various patterns and hierarchies, undergoing some modifications and transformations in particular parts of the work.

It seems to me that this type of composition – a limited number of elements with a variety of combinations, hierarchies and transformations, governed by a general principle of symmetry – is characteristic of more than just the composition of *Labyrinth*. Perhaps this compositional pattern could be discovered in some other works of ancient and medieval literature; perhaps it even indicates some links between the structure of 'old' literature and that of other arts, especially music.

However, before any degree of validity could be claimed for this hypothesis, a much deeper and systematic structural analysis of ancient and medieval literature and art in general would have to be accomplished. It is obvious that a structural description of one work of literature represents no more than a preliminary step in this historical investigation.[23] Nevertheless I believe that even a purely synchronous analysis of one literary work provides information not only about the specific work but about structural and stylistic principles generally; it can reveal clues that enable us to formulate hypotheses about literary structures of entire epochs and about the general trends of their evolution.

---

23 For more about the relationship of synchronous and diachronous (historical) study of literature see F. Vodička, 'Literární historie. Její problémy a úkoly' [Literary history. Its Problems and Tasks] in *Čtení o jazyce a poesii* [Readings in Language and Poetry], Prague, 1942, esp. pp. 344–55.

Scheme 1

P Pilgrim
P' Solomon
C Interpreters
C' Christ
W World
W' World of Christians

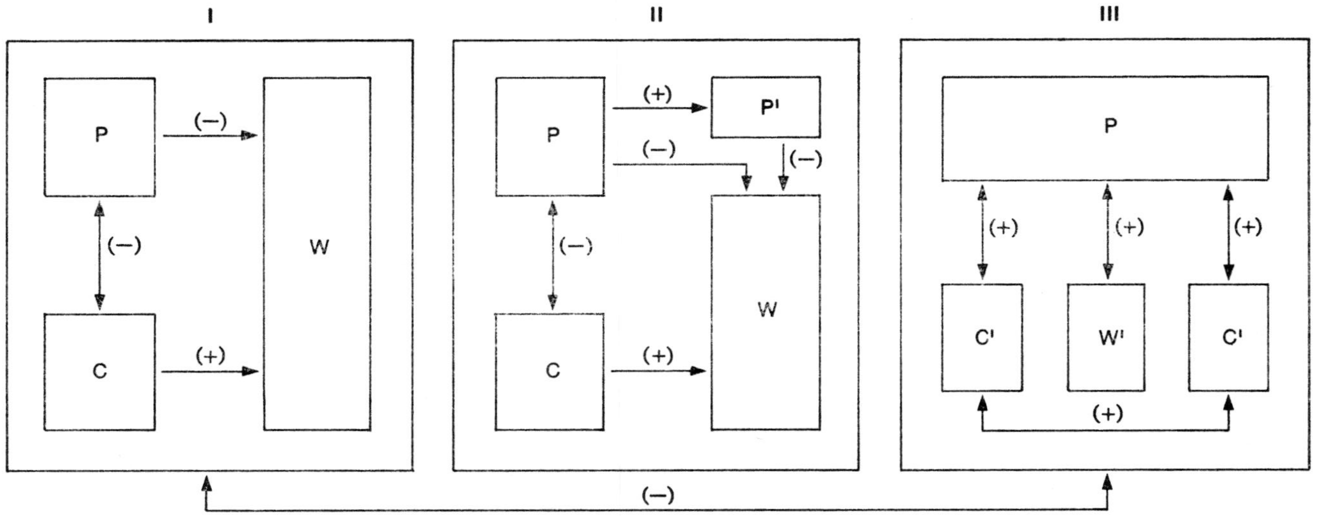

I

III

II

P (–) W negative rhetoric
C (+) W positive rhetoric
P (–) C dispute

P (+) P' substitution

P (+) C' 'friendly' dialogue
P (+) W' positive rhetoric
PC'(+) PW' (+) PC' secondary symmetry
I (–) III negative parallelism

3

The objective narrator: *Kaliba's Crime* by Karel V. Rais

Objective narrative, implementing the norms of the referent-oriented text, is a base of the theory and classification of narrative modes. At the same time, however, elementary misrepresentations of its nature and effect can be found in literary criticism; they result, probably, from the fact that it is difficult for a literary critic to accept the idea that a personal, partial and idiosyncratic author can incorporate in his text a 'discourse without speaker'. Therefore, with respect to the objective narrator, the basic assumption of the structural theory of narrative modes must be spelled out with special emphasis: the narrator is no 'deputy' of the author in the narrative text; rather it is a *narrative technique* created and applied by the author more or less consciously and consistently.

Two more introductory comments are necessary to dispense with some of the misunderstandings connected with the objective narrative mode:
1 It is inadmissible to identify the total effect of a piece of fiction with the effect produced by the narrator. The narrator is just one of many components of the fictional structure. The overall effect of the fictional work, i.e. the set of aesthetic, moral, philosophical, ideological preferences ('values') is generated by all the structural components in their contrasts and harmonies. Therefore, we can imagine a narrative work which employs the mode of the objective narrator, but which, in its total effect, generates partial and unequivocal value preferences. On the other hand, a fictional work is possible where the narrator is partial and idiosyncratic, but which generates a final effect of uncertainty or ambiguity of value preferences. The first case is well known from realistic fiction of the nineteenth century, the

second from romantic and modern fiction, especially because of 'narrative irony'.[1]

2 The objective narrator is a mode without the interpretative and action functions. However, the controlling and representational functions are not affected by the lack of secondary functions. In other words, a piece of fiction employing the technique of the objective narrator is not prose without narrator, but only prose without the interpreting and acting narrator.[2] Any statement about the 'death of the narrator' is a misleading rhetorical figure of speech.

In the search for a suitable example of a novel with an objective narrator, we naturally turn to that period which made the principle of impartiality and objectivity an essential part of its poetics, i.e. to the mature realism of the nineteenth century. It is to be emphasized that there is no necessary contingency between the style of realism and the mode of the objective narrator; rhetorical *Er*-form as well as various kinds of the *Ich*-form narrative are quite common in realistic fiction. Nevertheless, it can be expected that the aesthetic ideals of realism will lead to attempts at implementing the norms of the objective narrator in a rather systematic and consistent way.

In nineteenth-century Czech literature, an essential contribution to the development of the objective technique had been made by Božena Němcová; only occasionally does her narrative bear traces of sentimentalism and rhetoric. However, sentimentalism and rhetoric prevented Czech prose for a long time from adopting the technique of the objective narrator systematically and consistently. Only at the end of the nineteenth century did the Czech realistic and naturalistic novel materialize the ideal of objective representation.[3] One of the prominent representatives of the mature stage of Czech realism is Karel Václav Rais (1859–1926); his novel *Kaliba's*

1 'The narrative situation is ... ineluctably ironical ... Narrative irony is a function of disparity among ... (narrative) viewpoints.' (R. Scholes, R. Kellogg, *The Nature of Narrative*, London – Oxford – New York, 1966, p. 240.)

2 In this respect, I agree with W. Kayser who assumes that 'a narrator is present in all works of the narrative art.' ('Wer erzählt den Roman?' in *Die Vortragsreise. Studien zur Literatur*, Bern, 1958, p. 90.)

3 See J. Janáčková, *Český román na sklonku 19. století* [The Czech Novel at the End of the Nineteenth Century], Prague, 1967. The same author observes that even the most important representative of Czech realism in the historical novel, Alois Jirásek (1851–1930), does not follow the ideal of 'impersonal stylization'; rather, he creates a narrative 'subjectively biased', a narrative with 'personal tone and intimate emphasis'. (J. Janáčková, 'Jiráskovo vypravěčství, jeho charakter a funkce' [Jirásek's Narrative Art, Its Character and Functions], *Česká literatura*, xv (1967), p. 310.)

Crime (*Kalibův zločin*, 1892) offers very interesting material for the study of the objective narrator.[4]

Kaliba's Crime is a family tragedy set in a village of northern Bohemia. Farmer Vojta Kaliba, a shy, passive and hard-working man, marries a much younger girl, Karla, who has been deserted by her lover. After awhile, Karla and her mother provoke Kaliba into committing a desperate deed: in a fit of jealousy he kills his wife and dies shortly afterwards.

This brief outline of the story was given to show that the distribution of 'good' and 'evil' is quite obvious in Kaliba's tragedy. However, the narrator of *Kaliba's Crime* is strictly committed to impartiality and detachment. I was able to find only one instance where the norm of the objective narrator seems to be violated, the use of an evaluative adjective in the description of Karla's mother: 'the *repulsive* features of her face began to soften' [p. 177].

With the interpretative function of the narrator reduced to nil, the representational function asserts itself with even more vigour and strictness in *Kaliba's Crime*. It is responsible for the simple and well-defined arrangement of structural components which is typical for this type of novel.

The basic antinomy in the structure of *Kaliba's Crime* is the antinomy of two temporal planes, that of natural time and that of human time. Natural time, controlling the change of the seasons and the rhythm of the peasants' work, is *cyclical*; significantly, it is dated by indications taken from the traditional calendar of the peasant. In the arrangement of the natural time plane, *Kaliba's Crime* repeats the structure of the rural chronicle which is a favourite genre of Czech realists.

However, the time of human actions is no longer controlled by natural time; on the contrary, it follows its own *linear* curve. Moreover, human time is not 'synchronized' with the natural time: Kaliba's wooing coincides with 'the melancholy autumn' [p. 24], his wedding takes place on a cloudy day in late fall [p. 73]; he moves his young wife to their new home through the frozen immobility of a snow-covered winter landscape [p. 77–8]; the family conflict comes to the surface in spring when nature is full of 'the glare of sun' [p. 166]. Only the crisis and tragic dénouement of the human story become harmonized with natural time: the final disintegration of Kaliba's marriage is paralleled by the image of the gloomy nature of late

4 Shortly after its publication, *Kaliba's Crime* was translated into Russian, Danish and German; in English, of all Rais's prosaic works, only one short story 'The Newspaper' is available in Jeanne W. Němcová (ed. and transl.), *Czech and Slovak Short Stories*, London, 1967. All references in our text are made to the 12th edition of *Kaliba's Crime* in Spisy Karla V. Raise, Prague, 1937.

fall [p. 203], and the crime occurs during a winter night full of 'snow whiteness' and 'black darkness' [p. 232].

Even with this merging of natural and human time, the plane of natural events does not become a mere background for human actions, but preserves its autonomy. It is introduced in the same detailed and systematic manner as the plane of human actions. Moreover, in the succession of segments of the plane of nature and that of human actions, those of nature have a clear priority; quite often the chapter opens with a nature description; sometimes this description follows a brief introductory representation of the human action, but always precedes the core of the human-action representation.

The opposition between the plane of nature and the plane of human action is marked by an important formal distinction: motifs of the former plane are introduced in the narrative, whereas motifs of the latter come predominantly in the characters' speech (in the dramatic form of dialogues). Fully and exclusively controlling the plane of nature, the narrator designs the representation of nature so as to achieve maximal dynamism and variability; stylistic dynamism manifests itself in the texture of the particular landscapes; the variety can be observed when comparing several landscapes belonging to various periods of natural time:

1/ FALL: Bright clouds traversed a blue sky that shone paler and paler as it neared the sun; whenever a cloudlet sailed across the sun, whenever the others approached it, the light on the landscape shifted, shadows sprang up and transformed even the colours of the old forest. Now everything grew dark, now some light spots sparkled here and there. The green, brown, yellow hues exhibited all their variations.

WINTER: The masses of snow clouds dispersed and the blue sky arched over the earth. The sun quivered in the bright azure, but the hilly landscape was all in the whiteness of snow which the earth, once again frozen to the bone, still huddled under.

SPRING: The horizon stood out high and sharp. Over the soft-turned earth of the fields, larks sang and a flock of pigeons, white and ginger and dun, hovered in the air, their wings gleaming in the sunlight. Ash-grey crows strutted along the furrow and black ravens, with worn and whitish bills, pecked at the topsoil. A mild easterly breeze was rapidly drying the soggy tillage, the roads, the meadows and making the sparse woods flutter.

A combination of various stylistic devices is used to overcome the traditional static character of 'landscapes'. In this treatment, descriptions of nature are truly transformed into *a story of nature*, no less detailed, dynamic and variable than the human story rendered in the novel. As a result, the natural plane becomes an autonomous and equipotent contrast to the plane of human actions.

Another important component of the realistic novel is also under the exclusive control of the narrator: the external characterization (portrayal) of characters. Again, in this type of novelistic structure, motifs of external portrayal are much more than just secondary accessories of characters. The art of portrayal is an autonomous and important part of the realist's literary technique. Each character, whatever his importance in the development of the story, is described in all the details of face, figure and dress. This is a splendid opportunity for the objective narrator to render the variety of human outward appearance which in this presentation seems to be as much a part of nature as the landscape. This quality of realistic portrayal is emphasized by a meticulous avoidance of any correlation between outward traits and interior qualities of characters; this implies, furthermore, that the portrayal has no connection with the role of the character in the story. If we compare, for example, the portrayal of Vojtěch Kaliba with the portrayal of Karla's mother, we are unable to read into them anything about the mental and moral makeup of these characters or about their contrasting roles in the development of the tragedy:

2/ KALIBA: Young Kaliba, tall, strong, square-shouldered, stood, leaning against the door-post; he looked about thirty-five. On his mighty round head lay disarrayed locks of soft, chestnut-coloured hair; he had a low forehead with deep grooves and large blue, slightly bulging eyes. His face was full, ruddy with good health, and sun-tanned. He was dressed in a short woollen jacket, his trousers were tucked in tall, worn-out boots.

KARLA'S MOTHER: She was still a sturdy, healthy matron, although her face and forehead were greatly lined with wrinkles. She was dressed in a dark-coloured jacket and a short striped worsted skirt under which white stockings and velvet shoes could be seen. She had a kerchief on her head, knotted at the back of her head, her black hair was parted at the temples. When smiling, she showed that there were only a few strong teeth left in her mouth.

It seems to me that only in one detail – in the description of eyes – Rais's narrator waives the autonomy of the external portrayal and hints at a connection between the physiognomy and the interior makeup of characters.

As if following a popular Czech saying – 'The eye is the window of the soul' – the narrator renders flashes of interior life by describing the expression of the eyes. Thus, for example, in portrayals of the Kaliba family, given in the first chapter, each member is briefly characterized by the detail of his eyes or his look; this detail is clearly significant with respect to a constant or momentary mental quality. The device is especially apparent in the portrayal of Kaliba's future wife Karla:

3/ She was pretty, only her eyes occasionally flashed in a strange manner, her eyelashes frowning and her look acquiring a strange, wild, almost ugly expression, reminiscent of her mother.

Here, of course, the detail of portrayal is transformed into a clear indication of the future conflict in which Karla and her mother will play very similar roles.

Another similarity between the representation of nature and the portrayal of characters in *Kaliba's Crime* is the similarity in the position of their introduction. The portrait of a character is given immediately after the character enters the scene, before he gets involved in the dramatic action. (If there is a short speech uttered by the character before his portrayal, it is, as a rule, a purely formal phrase such as a greeting.) Because of the fixed place of the portrayal, one single deviation from the standard – Karla's portrayal – has a particularly surprising effect. This portrait is 'delayed'. There is a short scene inserted between Karla's entry and her portrayal. In this scene, Karla's attractiveness is commented on in a brief utterance by a secondary character and, significantly, in a brief interior monologue of Kaliba's. In other words, before the objective portrayal of Karla is presented, subjective impressions and evaluations of Karla's physical appearance are rendered. By emphasizing the very beginning of Kaliba's admiration for Karla, the device of 'delayed' portrayal acquires an important function in the development of the story.

Adding to these considerations a few traditional descriptions of interiors which need not be discussed here, we are now able to make a general statement about the main structural domain which in *Kaliba's Crime* is under the full and exclusive control of the objective narrator: it is the domain of the 'exterior world', of physical appearances of both the inanimate (landscapes, interiors), and the animate (characters) objects introduced into the novel. Because of the narrator's exclusive control, the plane of the 'exterior world' is kept strictly separated from the plane of human actions and their psychological motivations. The 'physicalism' of the objective narrator seems to be one of his most essential features; it defines the historical place of this mode with respect to other narrative modes and styles, committed to a different treatment of the relationship between the physical world and the human consciousness in fiction.[5]

In opposition to the physical domain, controlled by the narrator, human actions and their interior motivations are controlled by the characters themselves; these motifs are represented primarily in the characters' speech, in 'dramatic' self-revelation. Only in a few exceptional cases, which will be specified later, can the narrator be observed trespassing into this domain of the characters.

The action of *Kaliba's Crime* arises from changing relationships of the three protagonists; therefore, revelations of their psychology, of their attitudes and emotions, are necessary to motivate the action. The basic form in which psychological motivations are given is the self-revealing dialogue. The presentation of Karla's interior motivations is a good example of this function of the dialogue. Karla's emotional life remains hidden for a long time and we are not given any explanation for her strange behaviour toward her husband. Only later, in an agitated dialogue with her mother [p. 178], Karla reveals the external and internal motives which led to her marriage with Kaliba and to her present feelings of repulsion.

Preference for dialogue as a form of self-revelation is quite obvious in *Kaliba's Crime*. However, in one important exception, in the presentation of Kaliba's interior life, dialogue loses its monopoly. This circumstance can perhaps be related to Kaliba's character: he is a taciturn man who feels strong inhibitions against revealing his psychological states, especially in moments of crisis. There is, however, a more essential, purely structural reason for the exceptional treatment of Kaliba's interior life, namely his prominent position among the protagonists. Kaliba's interior motivations are especially important and, therefore, all the forms of their presentation are mobilized: Kaliba's participation in dialogues, his interior monologues and even the narrator's representation of Kaliba's psychology. It is here that the narrator commits his most serious 'trespassing', without, however, giving up his objectivity. The specificity of Kaliba's interior characterization consists in *the combination of numerous interior monologues with the psychological analysis expressed by the narrator*. Only quite rarely and in

---

5 I am leaving aside one important aspect of narrator's control of the 'exterior world', the use of devices organizing various descriptive components in higher units. Prominent among these devices is the method of gradual approach ('zooming') which is demonstrated in the very opening of the novel: natural environment – village – Kaliba's house – Kaliba family in the room – particular members of the family. Descriptions of the room are given simultaneously with the portrayal of the members of the Kaliba family.

minor instances are these two forms employed for the interior characterization of the other protagonists.[6]

A coupling of analytical narrative with self-revealing interior monologue is typical for the technique of Kaliba's interior characterization. A pattern where interior monologue, expressed in represented discourse, grows smoothly out of the narrative (see here, p. 48) was already known to Rais:

4/ But Vojta was ill-humoured; things had gotten a bit too much since yesterday; he wasn't used to it and didn't know how to get out from under. His dad, Nana, his mother-in-law – he was being bombarded from all sides. He had never been in such a fix before!

Here and there more complicated patterns of the coupling can be found, using both direct and represented discourse for the expression of the interior monologue:

5/ An evil thought flashed through his [Vojta's] mind. 'Perhaps, that soldier, Rachota, is there – why else wouldn't they have come back?' He had hardly given him a thought for a long time – but why, why wouldn't they come back? At the thought he clenched his fists, breathed heavily, could not stand still.

One more important device is used to emphasize Kaliba's prominence among the protagonists: he is the only character who lives and acts in both temporal planes of the novel, in the human, as well as in natural time. He is the only link connecting the two, otherwise disconnected, alternative modes of existence. With respect to Kaliba, nature assumes a character-forming function, indirectly participating, especially in moments of high tension, in the presentation of his state of mind. It is characteristic that nature comes to Kaliba even in prison: 'as the surface of the water under a strong wind, as a snowy landscape after a storm' [p. 216]. The most intimate fusion of state of mind with nature is materialized in the scene of Kaliba's night-watch in the fields:

6/ But he [Vojta] did not fall asleep. ... The darkened dome of the sky, sparsely dotted with radiant flowers of stars, loomed over him like the casing of an

6 Concentration of devices of psychological characterization on the main protagonist was apparently a rather common method in the realistic novel: see, for example, the focus on Raskol'nikov in F.M. Dostoyevsky's *Crime and Punishment*.

horrendous bell at the heart of which he reposed ... Vojta kept looking up at the sky. Every now and again a gentle breeze passed over his face, as if lightly bathing it; this was a silent greeting of the old forest that several times breathed heavily in its dreams.

There is clearly a deeper meaning hinted at by this scene of nature's compassion for Vojta; he is liberated from the noise and chaos of finite human time and elevated to the calmness, order and rhythm of natural time.

As has been emphasized several times, the drama of human conflicts in *Kaliba's Crime* is brought about primarily in dialogic scenes, where the characters themselves move the action by their autonomous verbal behaviour. In the development of the action, the narrator assumes the secondary role of reporter of summarized action scenes which connect the dominant 'dramatic' scenes. This is, I feel, a typical role for the objective narrator in the structuring of the story. On the other hand, it should be pointed out that, in this narrative mode, the narrator's participation in the story-structuring can be meaningfully described in terms of *negative control*, i.e. in manipulations which eliminate certain motifs (or certain groups of motifs) from the chronological sequence completely, or temporarily. The notion of negative control seems to be rather important for the general theory of the narrator; for the description of the objective narrator, it assumes a special importance.

In *Kaliba's Crime* two instances of negative control deserve brief mention. Its first manifestation is the suppression of erotic motifs which, of course, in a drama of passion, jealousy and repulsion are expected to play an important role in the development of the action and in the characters' motivations. In the spirit of the puritanism of the epoch, however, erotic motifs are almost completely eliminated from *Kaliba's Crime*. Thus, for example, the scene of the wedding night is replaced by a sequence of dashes, after which motifs of a quite 'businesslike' character follow [p. 77]. Disregarding mere flashes of Kaliba's reminiscences, the whole novel provides just one short scene where the imbalance of Kaliba's and Karla's erotic attitudes is explicitly expressed [p. 188]. Moreover, dialogues of characters, which in the spirit of this novelistic type should reveal this intimate, decisive component of their motivations, are controlled by the same inhibitions as is the narrative. This suppression of erotic motifs creates an impression (especially for the modern reader) of quite unsatisfactory motivation of the erotic tragedy.

The second manifestation of narrator's negative control is of a different character. It is the device of 'postponement', whereby a motif is taken out of its proper place in the chronological sequence and introduced later, in a different context. Because the story structure of *Kaliba's Crime* is governed by the principle of strict chronology, the device of postponement is especially conspicuous. In the depiction of Kaliba's wedding, we are surprised by the omission of the ceremony in the church which, of course, represents the ritual climax of a village wedding. The church scene appears only in the last chapter, as a part of the sequence of Kaliba's reminiscences during his fateful way home from prison. Appearing after this stream of remembrances, the church scene acquires a significant function in the presentation of Kaliba's gradually increasing agitation; it generates a series of questions about Karla's motivations, questions which are given a surprising and shocking answer at the end.

In this sense, the church scene undergoes a functional transformation through the device of postponement; an action scene is transformed into a character-forming scene, contributing to the motivation of Kaliba's final outrage. The device of postponement is also a significant manifestation of the strict and consistent *linearity* of plot construction in *Kaliba's Crime*; rather than repeat a motif, introduced elsewhere, the narrator deletes it in the original sequence, even though an inexplicable gap is thus created.

This brief analysis of the objective narrator in *Kaliba's Crime* leaves many aspects of this narrative technique untouched; nevertheless, some general conclusions may be postulated. This narrative mode appears to be governed by rather strict norms which, on the one hand, prohibit any manifestation of the interpretative function, and, on the other hand, delineate clearly and precisely the domains of the narrator's representational function. It was demonstrated that the objective narrator exhibits his representational function in the following domains of novelistic structure:

1 The narrator exclusively controls the representation of the plane of nature; representation is organized to present the natural plane as an autonomous and equipotent contrast to the plane of human actions.

2 The narrator is charged with the introduction of the characters on the stage and with presenting their outward appearance. The art of realistic portrayal is applied to all characters, regardless of their importance in the story. Therefore, character portrayal becomes another autonomous component of the novelistic structure.

3 The narrator takes upon himself, in combination with the interior monologue, the revelation of the interior makeup and the psychological motivations of Vojtěch Kaliba. By this focusing on his interior life, Kaliba acquires an exceptional prominence among the protagonists.

4 In the representation of the story, the narrator assumes only the secondary role of reporting summarized connecting actions. However, the narrator's negative control of the action representation makes itself felt by

elimination of erotic motifs and by the occasional use of the device of postponement.

5 Both in the sequence of natural time and in the structure of human time, strict chronology is enforced. Moreover, in the structure of human time the linear principle is at work, prohibiting any repetition of the same motif.

Much wider investigation will be needed, of course, before certain general conclusions about the *historical* aspects of the objective narrator in Czech fiction can be made. Let us repeat here that this narrative technique reached its perfection only at the end of the nineteenth century; this means that simultaneous with its culmination, it met its denial, its rejection by the subjectivistic tendencies of the *fin-de-siècle*. It seems to me that this specific situation in Czech fiction shows, in a rather dramatic manner, the historic transience of the objective narrative mode in general. The objective narrator (at least in the context of European fiction of the nineteenth century) seems to have been a relatively brief historical experience, establishing itself between the rhetorical tendencies of older romantic fiction and the subjectivistic trends of modern narrative. The subjectivistic trends manifest themselves in the narrative activation of characters, leading, on the one hand, to a high frequency of the personal *Ich*-form, and on the other hand, to the establishment of the subjective *Er*-form. Moreover, it should be taken into account that the origins of the subjective mode are not to be sought in twentieth-century fiction, but rather in the very core of nineteenth-century realism.[7]

The transient character of the objective narrative technique is further determined by the fact that this narrative mode can be materialized only within the framework of the traditional narrative text (cf. here, pp. 17–18, 93). Only in a structure of this type (recognized by strict boundaries between narrative and characters' speech) can the objective narrative preserve its 'purity', protected from any influence coming from the speech of characters.

It is interesting to discover that the novel *Kaliba's Crime* offers a surprising view of the transformation of the traditional narrative text into the modern one. In conspicuous contrast to all the preceding chapters, the last chapter of *Kaliba's Crime* develops certain devices which point to the new

---

7 Important stages in the development of this narrative mode are, for example, quotations from the characters' utterances in the narrative in F.M. Dostoyevsky's novels and L.N. Tolstoy's narrative activation of characters in his implementation of the device of 'making strange' (cf. here, p. 120).

novelistic type.[8] In the depiction of Kaliba's journey from prison, we find a quite unusual sequence made up of Kaliba's reminiscences, beginning with a scene from his childhood and ending with the church scene of his wedding (already dealt with in another context, p. 87). Kaliba's reminiscences alternate with depictions of the winter landscape and this alternation is strongly reminiscent of a favourite device of modern fiction (cf., pp. 48–9, 106). There is, however, a substantial formal difference: Kaliba's reminiscences are not expressed in the form of a spontaneous interior monologue (as we expect in modern fiction), but are transformed into the descriptive form of narrative.

Immediately after this sequence of reminiscences, a second passage employs the device of presenting alternately the 'interior state' of the character and the 'outward world' of nature. This time, the interior state is represented by Kaliba's repeated painful question and given in the form of an interior monologue; however, this monologue still uses the traditional form of expression – direct discourse.

Thus, it seems apparent that the 'modern' confrontation of exterior world and of interior human experience (consciousness) is carried out with surprising originality but, at the same time, is kept within the forms of the traditional narrative text.

In the culmination of the chapter which represents the dramatic dénouement of the story, Rais spontaneously discovers the most conspicuous device of modern narrative text, the subjective *Er*-form. Several DC signals (cf. here, pp. 52–3) can easily be detected in the representation of the scene of Kaliba's arrival at his house (italics mine – LD):

7/ Vojta stood behind his house. ... – *Here* is the barn – gleaming *over there* is the wall of *father's* cottage. ... – The cottage is *so sad*, dark – and on the other side, in the farmhouse, it *will be just the same anyhow*. ... He hurried across the yard, leaned against the old apple-tree that veered toward the roof above the room and, as if in welcome, showered him with white flowers of snow. – Standing on tip-toe, inclining his body forward, he gazed into the room. ... *There!* on a bench, under the other window *sits* his mother-in-law and she laughs, she laughs noisily and her eyes glitter. – One step closer and Vojta was standing at the very wall. ... – For an instant, he caught sight of

---

8 The exceptional status of the last chapter is emphasized by a short epilogue which, as it were, expresses mistrust of the objective narrator: the epilogue offers an interpretation of Kaliba's desperate deed and an explicit moral message, expressed, however, by the 'voice of the people' rather than by the narrator.

Karla – she was saying *something*, but not to her mother – *somebody* else was *there*.

This scene where Kaliba's interior state fuses indistinguishably with the exterior action, as observed by him, is quite exceptional in *Kaliba's Crime*. At the same time, it is an important document of the origins of the subjective *Er*-form mode in Czech fiction. It leads us to assume that the transformation of the traditional narrative text into the modern one is a qualitative process in a quantitative form. First, a 'modern' device appears within the traditional text as an occasional exception, employed only to solve an exceptional task of representation (a scene of high 'interior' dramatism). In time, the exceptional device becomes more and more frequent and, finally, the exception establishes itself in the position of a norm. When this occurs, the transformation of the old structural type into the new one is completed.

4

Karel Čapek and Vladislav Vančura: An essay in comparative stylistics

Stylistics, as its history well illustrates, aims not only at studying specific features of a particular literary work or author, but also at investigating the general properties of special groups or classes of literary works. Terms such as 'genre style', 'period style', 'style of a literary school', for example, attest to these generalizing tendencies.[1] What has proved to be the essential tool in stylistic study both on the specific and general levels is the comparative method; by comparing various literary structures, stylistics can reveal what is common to them all, and what constitutes their differences.

One of the most interesting results of comparative stylistics is the revelation of an unsuspected similarity, of a hidden kinship of two stylistic systems which, on the surface, seem to be contradictory. This was the goal aimed at by Jan Mukařovský in his comparative investigation of two typical, but antagonistic, representatives of Czech romantic poetry, Karel Hynek Mácha (1810–36) and Karel Jaromír Erben (1811–70).[2] Mukařovský confirmed the impression of a 'contradiction between the fundamental semantic tendencies in Erben's and Mácha's styles' that readers and critics had felt. At the same time, however, he asserted that the contrasting semantic tendencies had the 'common background' of a tendency toward the 'individualization of the thing expressed by the verbal means'. The

1 L.T. Milic's objections to a typology of styles (in S. Chatman, S.R. Levin (eds.), *Essays on the Language of Literature*, Boston, 1967, pp. 442–50) seem to be relevant with respect to methods applied in Anglo-American literary criticism and to ambiguous results obtained by these methods rather than with respect to a possibility of a typology of styles.

2 J. Mukařovský, 'Protichůdci' [Antipodes], *Slovo a slovesnost*, II (1936), pp. 33–43.

stylistic contrast between Mácha and Erben arises because this general tendency is implemented in opposite ways: 'Mácha strives for individualization in time, whereas Erben for that in space. Together with its focus on time, Mácha's style tends to veil objectiveness and emphasize motion, whereas Erben, on the contrary, intensifies objectiveness.'[3]

Felix Vodička proceeded in much the same way when investigating the common background of two stylistic poles in Czech pre-romantic poetry; these poles are represented, on the one hand, by the 'lofty and innovative pathos' of the poetry of Jan Kollár (1793–1852) and, on the other hand, by the 'poeticization of the folk element' in the poetry of František Ladislav Čelakovský (1799–1852). 'The common historical background,' writes Vodička, 'is in both cases the tendency toward poetry with focus on verbal means, distinctly different from the established and canonized devices of everyday, rationalized speech with its dominant tendency toward communicative definiteness.'[4]

The quotation from Vodička contains in essence one of the fundamental theses of the Prague structuralist school concerning the genesis and history of literary styles: a new literary style can be explained as the negation of a preceding, 'canonized' literary style; at the same time, the new style is amenable to a rich variety of individual manifestations with a wide range of idiosyncratic devices. This means that an investigation into historical background is necessary in order to reveal and to explain the general features and the individual diversity of a new literary style.

Just such a course will be followed in this essay: to demonstrate that the contrasting styles of two outstanding representatives of modern Czech fiction, Karel Čapek (1890–1938) and Vladislav Vančura (1891–1942),[5] can both be interpreted as negation of the same, historically preceding literary style, that of nineteenth-century realistic fiction. Because of their common historical base, Čapek's and Vančura's styles are dominated by features that reflect – in spite of their external contrast – an underlying kinship and similarity. We can say, borrowing the terminology of modern linguistics, that in their contrasting 'surface structure', Čapek's and Vančura's

3 *Ibid.*, p. 42.

4 F. Vodička, *Počátky krásné prózy novočeské* [The Beginnings of Modern Czech Belles-Lettres], Prague, 1948, p. 322.

5 Although the importance of Vančura's writings for the development of modern Czech prose fiction is, without doubt, equivalent to that of Čapek's, their popularity in the English-speaking world is extremely uneven. While practically all of Čapek's works (both prosaic and dramatic) were translated into English soon after their publication in Czech, only a handful of Vančura's works have appeared in English (some stories in anthologies of Czech literature and one novel, *The End of the Old Times*, separately).

styles are divergent manifestations of a common underlying 'deep structure' which, in turn, results from a negation of the 'deep structure' of traditional, realistic prose style.

To substantiate this general assumption, I would like to develop my argument in three successive steps: In section A, I will attempt a reconstruction of the fundamental 'deep structure' features of traditional fictional style. In section B, fundamental features of modern fictional style will be derived tentatively by a logical operation transforming the traditional features into the contrary; the features derived will be supposed to represent the sought 'deep structure' of Čapek's and Vančura's individual styles. In section C, an analysis of the 'surface structure' of Čapek's and Vančura's styles will be undertaken in order to demonstrate that these contrasting styles are divergent manifestations of the same 'deep structure'.

A FUNDAMENTAL FEATURES OF TRADITIONAL FICTIONAL STYLE

In keeping with the aims and scope of this study, I must limit myself to a mere sketch of three fundamental features of the traditional fictional style which are most relevant for our investigation: the opposition of the narrator's discourse (DN) (narrative) and the characters' discourse (DC), the objective narrator, and the semantic homogeneity of narrative.

1 The traditional style of prose fiction manifests itself within the framework of the traditional narrative text; this means that it is marked by a strict and explicit distinction between DN and DC. Specifically, a text of traditional style is made up of clearly delimited segments of narrative and of dialogues (or some rare monologues) of acting characters, the latter expressed in the form of direct discourse. The opposition is materialized by accumulation of binary discriminative features and, in addition, by conventional graphic signs of delimitation (cf. here, pp. 17–18).

One of the most conspicuous discriminative features, differentiating DN from DC, is the opposition of speech levels. In realistic Czech prose fiction of the nineteenth century, this opposition is implemented by the narrative being based on the unspecified, 'neutral' speech level, reflecting the norm of contemporary standard Czech, whereas the utterances of characters are directed toward spoken, colloquial Czech of the period; quite often, characters' discourse tends toward substandard forms, especially toward regional dialects.[6] Moreover, disregarding some substandard 'quotations'

---

6 Cf. A. Jedlička, 'Spisovný jazyk a nářečí v Mrštíkově *Roku na vsi*' [Standard Language and Dialect in Mrštík's *A Year in the Village*] in *Pocta Fr. Trávníčkovi a Fr. Wollmanovi*, Brno, 1948, p. 187.

(usually enclosed in quotation marks), traditional narrative is homogeneous with respect to its speech level. On the contrary, speech manners of various characters are usually differentiated by employing different variants and layers of spoken Czech. This is the basis for a favourite device of realistic fiction – *speech characterization*; a correlation exists between the character's characterology, i.e. the set of his depicted properties, and his speech characteristic, i.e. his idiosyncratic manner of speaking. I would suggest designating this literary device the *motivated* speech characterization.[7]

2 The second fundamental feature of the traditional fictional style implied in the first feature is the 'objectivity' and 'passivity' of the narrator. A detailed analysis of this narrative mode was given in the preceding essay of this collection; here, let us only emphasize the 'passivity' of the objective narrator which was pointed to by Jan Mukařovský: 'All facts, both "material" and psychological are introduced to the reader as if he directly "saw" them. For the narrator there remains – of course only ostensibly – at the very best the role of the objective of a camera or of an exactly recording scientific apparatus.'[8]

This characterization of the objective narrator applies fully to the third-person narrative only (*Er*-form); first-person narrative (*Ich*-form) defies this description. It is obvious that by its very nature the *Ich*-form displays a 'personalized' narrator rather than an anonymous reporter. However, the evidence available (no history of the *Ich*-form in Czech literature has been written) indicates that the traditional *Ich*-form has some features that bring it close to the objective *Er*-form narrative. First of all, *Ich*-form apparently plays a secondary role in Czech realistic fiction; the dominant form of narrative is the *Er*-form. It is to be assumed that the objectifying tendency of the traditional realistic style is responsible for this hierarchy of the two forms. Secondly, the pressure of objectification seems to have made the *observer's form* prominent among all *Ich*-form variants. In this form, a 'personalized' narrator is introduced; at the same time, he lacks the interpretative and action functions. Thus, observer's *Ich*-form is just a

7 An interesting example of socially motivated speech characterization is provided by Božena Němcová's story The Mountain Village (*Pohorská vesnice*, 1856). The peasants speak a south-western Czech dialect (of the region called Chodsko); the itinerant Slovak tinkers bring with them the Slovak dialect of their home region; the handicraftsmen make use of the spoken standard Czech of that period, whereas some representatives of the aristocracy tint the standard Czech with a rather strong archaic and bookish colouring.

8 J. Mukařovský, 'Vývoj Čapkovy prózy' [The Evolution of Čapek's Prose] in *Kapitoly z české poetiky*, Prague, 1948, vol. II, p. 329.

formal variant of the objective *Er*-form. By presenting 'documents of life', it enhances the illusion of objectivity.[9] In the observer's variant, the *Ich*-form narrative is prevented from developing its inherent subjectivism.

3 It has been stated in A1 that the narrative of the traditional text is homogeneous in its speech level, abstaining from speech-level contrasts and shifts. Even if the narrative, for certain reasons, should deviate from the neutral literary standard (as, for example, in historical novels with their tendency to archaize narrative style), such a deviation is consistent and the special speech level is preserved throughout the whole work.

Here let us briefly describe another fundamental quality of the traditional narrative: its *semantic homogeneity*. We can claim that semantic homogeneity of narrative is closely related to the objectivity of the narrator, as described in A2. In order to create the illusion of a detached 'report', the language of the narrative has to be *referential* in its nature.[10] The verbal expression of the 'report' has to avoid being conspicuous, attracting attention to itself; it is expected to be a transparent medium of narrated events. In accordance with the norms of referential language, traditional narrative prefers conventional means of expression and conventional modes of semantic concatenation. The context of narrative is built of semantically congruent units; their concatenation is governed by conventional semantic norms. Even rhetorical figures, if used, tend to be stereotyped, recurrent, and therefore inconspicuous.

It was Samuel T. Coleridge who very early pointed to the referential nature of prosaic language as distinct from the language of poetry. He wrote: 'The definition of good prose is – proper words in their proper places; of good verse – the most proper words in their proper places. The propriety is in either case relative. The words in prose ought to express the intended meaning, and no more; if they attract attention to themselves, it is, in general, a fault. ... But in verse you must do more: there the words, the *media* must be beautiful, and ought to attract your notice – yet not so much and so perpetually as to destroy the unity which ought to result from the whole poem.'[11] Coleridge's 'prosaic principle' is still professed by many critics, although it has long been overcome by the later development of fiction.

---

9 Cf. the analysis of Pushkin's *Belkin Tales* in V.V. Vinogradov's monograph *Stil' Puškina* [Pushkin's Style], Moscow, 1941.

10 This statement is slightly different in wording, but generally equivalent to our definition of narrative (in the traditional narrative text) as referent-oriented text (see here, pp. 16–17).

11 S. T. Coleridge, 'Table Talk' in St. Potter (ed.), *Select Poetry and Prose*, London, 1933, p. 512–3.

These are, in brief, the fundamental characteristic traits of the traditional prose fiction style which are relevant for our investigation. I would like to repeat once more that all of these traits are norms in the typological sense only: they are general tendencies which in particular works of fiction are or can be implemented with some degree of inconsistency and with a certain latitude for deviations.

B   FUNDAMENTAL FEATURES OF MODERN FICTIONAL STYLE

The traditional style of prose fiction disintegrated in a long historical process and was replaced by a new modern prosaic style. For our purposes, there is no need to describe the complex history of its rise; rather we will try to deduce its fundamental features in a purely logical way. The traditional features just described will be transformed to the contrary; thereby we hope to arrive at a frame of reference for the description of various individual styles in modern Czech fiction.

1 The opposition and clear-cut differentiation of the narrator's discourse (DN) and the characters' discourse (DC) will be replaced by a mutual assimilation and mixing of the two verbal planes. In the essay 'Represented Discourse in Modern Czech Narrative Prose' (see pp. 15–55), a detailed description of the forms and results of this essential transformation can be found. Here, we need dwell only briefly on one aspect of this transformation, namely on the dissolution of the opposition of speech levels (as defined in A1). Once the barrier between DN and DC is broken down, a free flow of verbal means from one plane to another becomes possible. This leads to various degrees of assimilation, interaction and mixture of the speech levels of the two planes. In an extreme case, both DN and DC can be based on one and the same speech level.

Because the verbal means of DC can freely penetrate into the narrative, the speech-level homogeneity of narrative cannot be retained. Even if a certain speech level represents the base of narrative, means of other speech levels can percolate into the base. Thus, speech-level shifts become common. Where traditional narrative preserved one 'timbre' throughout, modern narrative is free to alternate 'timbres' and to create changing stylistic blends.

2 The objectivity and passivity of the traditional narrator, outlined in A2 will be changed into the modern narrator's subjectivity and activity. Modern narrative will no longer pretend to be a 'report'. Instead of the authenticity of the 'report', the authenticity of the 'reporter' will become prominent. The narrator's ambition will not be to convey the narrated events as 'objectively' as possible, but rather to emphasize the specific, subjective

'distortion'. Narrated events will be analyzed from various subjective points of view. The narrator is no longer inhibited from expressing his likes and dislikes, his reactions and commentaries, his warnings and appeals.

The subjective narrator can appear in two specific modes of the third-person narrative, the *rhetorical* and *subjective Er*-form. It is only natural, however, that the first-person narrative (*Ich*-form) should become the most prominent form of the subjective narrator. In modern fiction the frequency of the *Ich*-form increases substantially; at the same time, the observer variant retires to a secondary position and the dominant role is taken over by the *personal Ich-form*: the narrator tells his own story and becomes engrossed in psychological motivations and reactions.

3 In B1 the transformation from the narrative homogeneous in its speech level to a narrative of speech-level shifts and contrasts has been outlined. Similarly, the semantic homogeneity of the narrative will be changed to the contrary. Repudiating the norms of referential language, modern narrative unloosens the relationship between the verbal sign and its referent and debars semantic conventions and stereotypes from having control over concatenation of verbal units. The verbal sign will be thrust into unusual contexts and thus will become 'strange', 'actualized'. Breaking down semantic limitations imposed by the norms of referential language, modern narrative is full of semantic surprises, shifts, contrasts. In such a way, modern fiction repudiates the 'prosaic principle' and associates itself rather with the 'poetic principle', with all the consequences brought about by this fundamental change, including a seeming self-destruction.

In the introduction to this essay, we associated ourselves with the idea of the Prague school that a new literary style can be explained as a negation, a 'negative transform' of its historical base. We assume therefore that the features derived in B1, B2, and B3 represent the sought 'deep structure' of modern fictional style. It now must be shown that Karel Čapek's and Vladislav Vančura's individual styles can indeed be related to this common 'deep structure'.

C 'SURFACE STRUCTURE' OF ČAPEK'S AND VANČURA'S STYLES

1 Both Čapek and Vančura repudiate the traditional speech-level differentiation of DN and DC. However, their implementations of this general feature go in opposite directions: Čapek assimilates narrative to characters' discourse, whereas in Vančura's fiction, characters' discourse is adjusted to the speech level of narrative. Moreover, Vančura shifts his narrative strongly towards a bookish, biblical base, so that, in the final outcome, the whole text is characterized by unusual archaization and loftiness. On the

contrary, the end-product of Čapek's technique is a piece of fiction dominated by colloquial language, giving the impression of spontaneous, oral story-telling.

Čapek's narrative style can be best understood in the light of his own characterization of the *prime story-telling situation* (specified with regard to the folk tale): 'A true folk fairy-tale does not originate in being taken down by the collector of folklore but in being told by a grandmother to her grandchildren, or by one member of the Yoruba tribe to other members of the Yoruba tribe, or by a professional story-teller to his audience in an Arab coffee-house. A real fairy-tale, a fairy-tale in its true function is a tale within a circle of listeners. The discovery of writing and printing has estranged us from this original and ancient delight: no longer do we sit in a circle hanging onto the lips of an expert story-teller; we read our newspapers or our books which deprive us of the pristine human urge to sit down together and let ourselves be quietly rocked by the spoken word. And so a true fairy-tale lives only where the written word has not become all powerful, with children and primitive people.'[12]

The spoken word of the story-teller is one fundamental component of the prime story-telling situation; the other, no less important, is the direct contact between the story-teller and his audience. Not only is there a 'feedback' from the audience to the story-teller, but the two roles are easily interchangeable: telling of stories can be passed on as a relay, because all listeners are potential story-tellers.

It was Čapek's ambition to recreate the delights of prime story-telling, of a 'tale within a circle of listeners'. Colloquial speech was the most adequate base and the first person was the best form for narrative of this type; allocutional devices provide a direct contact with a 'supposed' listener.

The best examples of this technique can be found in Čapek's lesser genres, such as short stories, fairy tales, travel sketches, essays, feuilletons, etc.[13] Among them, *Tales from the Other Pocket* (*Povídky z druhé kapsy*, 1929) are the most consistent in the effort to recreate the prime story-telling situation. Successively, one after another, participants of a gathering take over the function of narrator and contribute their story to the symposium. No wonder this cycle recalls such ancient predecessors as *Canter-*

12 K. Čapek, 'Towards a Theory of Fairy-Tales', English translation in *In Praise of Newspapers and Other Essays on the Margin of Literature*, London, 1951.
13 J. Mukařovský suggested Čapek's journalism as the source for the colloquial style of his minor genres (*Kapitoly z české poetiky*, vol. II, p. 346). However, the reverse is also possible: Čapek's journalism could have been under the influence of his oral story-telling. A typical journalistic style leans rather to rhetoric and formality.

bury Tales.[14] Čapek's style, however, is thoroughly modern, skilfully using various resources of contemporary spoken Czech. Čapek is well aware of the dominant position of professional languages and slangs in the system of contemporary spoken language; therefore, he differentiates his particular narrators, people of various professions, primarily by typical expressions of their profession, creating a spectrum of 'professional' *Ich*-narratives.

Here is a portion of a story told by a musician:

1/ Then two people came up, a man and a woman, but they didn't see me; they sat down with their backs to me and started talking in undertones. ... At the beginning, they talked very staccato; then the man began to explain something slowly and softly, as if he was at a loss for words; and then he shot his words quickly. The woman screamed with horror and spoke some agitated words to him; but he squeezed her hand till she moaned and began to urge something upon her, talking between his teeth. You know, this wasn't love talk, a musician can tell that; lover's persuasions have quite a different cadence and haven't got that tense sound about them – love talk is a deep cello, but this was a high bass, played in a sort of *presto rubato*, in a single key, as if the man kept repeating the same phrase. ... The woman began to cry softly ... her voice was a little like a clarinet, a reedy voice which didn't sound quite young. ... Then the man's voice started murmuring something in very low tones, a pure bass, almost amorously; the woman's crying passed over into short and passive sobs; that meant that her opposition had been overcome ...

This example indicates that professional language in Čapek's tales is more than a speech level of narrative; it is a direct and most adequate expression of a subjective narrator (see C2), conveying the narrated events with an inherent professional 'bias'. Musical terminology and phraseology are transformed into the narrator's phraseology, becoming the base of his metaphors, epithets, comparisons: *they talked very staccato; love talk is a deep cello; her voice was a little like a clarinet, a reedy voice,* etc. This is more than just professional speech level; this is a professional view of fictional reality, of the narrated events.

Ich-narrative, by its close affiliation with oral story-telling, offers the best opportunity for Čapek's masterly display of a wide range of colloquial

---

14 It is, however, characteristic of the *Tales from the Other Pocket* that the participants in the story-telling are not introduced and that no motivating frame or prologue is given. This indicates that Čapek strived at recreating the 'prime story-telling situation' by the stylistic devices of the narrative alone.

speech levels; however, the same proclivity for colloquial language is also strong in Čapek's *Er*-narratives. From the *Factory for the Absolute* (or *Absolute at Large*) (*Továrna na absolutno*, 1922) through *Krakatit* (1924) and *Tales from One Pocket* (*Povídky z jedné kapsy*, 1929) to *The War with the Newts* (*Válka s mloky*, 1936) and *The First Rescue Party* (*První parta*, 1937), Čapek's narrative is oriented toward modern colloquial Czech in its vocabulary, syntax and intonation.[15]

It is important to point to one function carried out by means of spoken language in Čapek's prose fiction: it is used to express 'stream-of-consciousness', to record a character's innermost thoughts and feelings before they have reached the level of orderly formulation. This function is carried out primarily by certain syntactic means, typical of spoken language, such as asyndetic coordination, ellipsis, anacoluthon, aposiopesis, etc. It can be assumed that spoken language syntax played a major role in the development of the modern stream-of-consciousness technique, and Čapek's novels exemplify this stage of the history of the technique.

Utilizing the social and (to a lesser degree) the regional differentiation of spoken Czech, Čapek preserves in most of his works motivated speech characterization (see A1). His characters, like his first-person narrators, manifest their social, professional, regional origins and personal history by their speech idiosyncrasies; however, special vocabulary as exemplified by Prokop's professional terminology (in *Krakatit*) or by Hordubal's Americanisms (in *Hordubal*) is just one ingredient in a character's speech. Čapek's best characters are multidimensional, and so is their speech.

Čapek's inclination toward spoken language is, in its general aspect, a continuation of the best traditions of nineteenth-century Czech literature. In the 1840s, attempts at bringing the language of prose (and, to a lesser extent, the language of poetry) closer to the spoken language of the period can be observed. It is a development described by the historians of Czech literary language as the 'democratization' of literary Czech. On the other hand, however, both the historical circumstances and the aims of the nineteenth-century 'democratization' were essentially different from the endeavours of Karel Čapek. The nineteenth-century process was aimed at closing a gap that existed between the language of literature (still based on sixteenth-century standards) and the cultivated language of the newly emerging Czech intelligentsia. With this process, the speech level of nar-

---

15 J. Mukařovský designated this quality of Čapek's narrative 'dialogic style': 'We have here, as a matter of fact, a continuous dialogue; speech is always addressed to somebody; it is a dialogue whose participants are not only the poet and the reader, but also the narrated characters and things' (*Kapitoly z české poetiky*, vol. II, p. 371).

rative in Czech realistic fiction became stylistically 'neutral' with respect to the contemporary cultivated standard; the characters' discourse then was opened to the influence of the colloquial or even substandard variants of spoken Czech (see A1). In Čapek's work, however, colloquial language becomes a base for a new narrative style, developing its own narrative devices and effects (cf. C3).

In any case, Čapek's mode of neutralizing the opposition between the speech levels of DN and DC is closer to nineteenth-century trends than that of Vančura; he returns to the past to base both his narrative and the utterances of his characters on an archaic, biblical language.[16] Vančura's early style is especially consistent in this respect, as the following passage from his novel *Jan Marhoul, the Baker* (*Pekař Jan Marhoul*, 1924) illustrates. Both Jan Marhoul and his wife Josefina express themselves in lofty style, conforming to the narrative environment:

2/ Now Josefina came and placing a cool hand upon his anger answered him:
   'All that you say, Jan, is little. When the door of this mill shall be opened, whither shall we go? Anger is but a moment, but board and lodging are long lasting. Jericho will not fall at a shout.'
   'The matter is decided,' said Jan, 'we shall not remain in Nadelhoty. It is time once again, Josefina, for us to take up our belongings and move to another place.'
   'I do not regret it,' answered she, 'but it will be no better elsewhere. We are poor and in all places we are destined to serve ...'

A direct consequence of the bookish speech level of DC is the abolition of motivated speech characterization; the consistent archaic speech level of both DN and DC does not allow for any idiosyncracy, for any individual deviation.[17] Thus, for example, in the novel *Tilled Fields and Battlefields*

---

16 Vančura, in his efforts to overcome the stylistic norms of realistic fiction, found many stimuli in pre-realistic fiction; his connections with the Renaissance period have often been mentioned; his links with 'romantic irony' should be added. The language of the Bible was obviously one of the major sources of Vančura's style; now, M. Grygar points also to some narrative devices of the Bible which are reflected in Vančura's fiction (M. Grygar, 'Bedeutungsgehalt und Sujetaufbau im *Pekař Jan Marhoul* von Vladislav Vančura', *Zeitschrift für Slawistik*, XIV (1969), p. 204f.).

17 A similar feature in modern Russian literature was described by I. Titunik: 'The individual peculiarities of speech of this or that personage, which ordinarily play so important a role in rendering reported speech in narrative fiction, have largely, if not completely, vanished, and all characters, notwithstanding their age, sex, social position, education, profession, nationality, etc., deliver themselves in exactly the same "lingo" as the narrator.' ('The Problem of "Skaz" in Russian Literature', PhD. dissertation, University of California, Berkeley, 1963, p. 115.)

(*Pole orná a válečná*, 1925), not only farm workers, but even the village idiot, Řeka, saturate their dialogues and interior monologues with biblical imagery, archaic vocabulary and complicated syntax. Here is an example of Řeka's speech manner:

3/ 'O riches! Riches above the longings of the heart! Each day I am punished and each day I pray. Our Father, who art in Heaven, give me the money and the treasures which thou art hiding. I will be fortunate like unto the proud and like unto the tyrant who beats me, although I give over to him the money which he claims. I will tell such things because I saw them when I entered the dwelling of the richest man ...'

The abolition of the motivated speech characterization represents a drastic deviation from the conventions of the traditional prose style. The 'natural' correlation which existed between a character's 'content' (make-up) and his 'form' (speech) and which gave the character aesthetic balance is destroyed. A character's verbal behaviour is no longer predictable on the basis of his 'characterology'. This variance between the expected and the materialized, between the 'natural' convention and a deviation from it, this is, of course, a typical device of 'making strange', of 'actualization' in the sense of those terms in formalistic poetics. In this interpretation, abolition of motivated speech characterization belongs to a whole group of devices of the 'making strange' variety which contribute to the specific 'poetic' quality of Vančura's fictional style.

Vančura, however, is not quite consistent in abolishing motivated speech characterization, especially in his later writings. Thus, for example, in *The End of the Old Times* (*Konec starých časů*, 1934), the speech of some characters appears to be socially or even regionally motivated. This holds true especially about the 'lower class' characters; the speech of domestics is oriented towards substandard 'common Czech' (*obecná čeština*) and similar verbal means appear also in a letter written by the narrator's sister; one of the maids (Veronika) makes use of forms of a Moravian dialect. Nevertheless, Vančura's technique seems to be rather different from the traditional motivated speech characterization. Firstly, substandard means are blended with verbal elements which are entirely out of keeping with the language of the people; secondly, in the speech of Váňa (a Russian servant), the expected russisms do not appear; instead, elements of 'common Czech' are interpolated into his speech. These observations lead to the conclusion that the ingredient of 'common Czech' is used in a compositional function, rather than for purposes of characterization: it distinguishes the domestics from the gentry, as two opposite groups of characters. The gentry group is marked by usage of lofty speech with archaic colouring and no attempt at individual specification; the peculiar feature of the domestic group consists in substandard forms which are only exceptionally differentiated with respect to the individual characters, and only partly motivated.

A rather interesting manifestation of the essential speech-level shift of narrative is Vančura's *Ich*-form. By its very nature, the speech level of an *Ich*-story is based on the speech of a character (functioning as narrator); it is (notwithstanding all possible modifications) a character's utterance promoted to the function of narrative. It is, therefore, not surprising that Vančura's *Ich*-form, in conformity with the general speech level of DC, tends to a bookish, archaic, biblical style. As a matter of fact, Vančura can be credited with creating the *bookish Ich-narrative* in modern Czech literature. In this respect, Vančura's first-person narrative is directly opposite to that of Čapek's. However, at the same time, there is a common background to this opposition. In his bookish *Ich*-form, Vančura makes every effort to bridge the gap between the narrator and his reader which is – as we know – the prime goal of Čapek's oral *Ich*-form. In order to create a narrative technique adequate to that purpose Vančura revives some devices of the Bible, of renaissance tales, of primitive story-telling. These devices, found also in Vančura's *Er*-form, will be dealt with briefly in C2.

Now let us just mention the best-known of Vančura's *Ich*-narratives, *The End of the Old Times*. Told by a retired (or, rather, dismissed) librarian by the name of Spera, it is a chronicle of the end of the old nobility and of the coming of the new, vulgar gentry after World War I. Its archaic style, reminiscent of the style of old chronicles, arises from a combination of archaic means of various linguistic levels – morphological, syntactic and lexical. Archaic Czech grammatical forms and syntactic structures, which defy translation, are still understandable to a native speaker, but they produce an effect of a rather artificial style:

4/ I did not give ear to her in this matter, but now that I am old, I wot that her counsels held a grain of wisdom.

On returning home, I disrobed and made ready for bed.

And having spoken those things, she fled, not tarrying for an answer.

The overall lofty and archaic tone of Spera's narrative is reinforced by abstract imagery, poeticisms and archaic pejoratives. It is generally true that Vančura's tongue-lashing is always archaic. (Characteristically, Van-

čura himself considered curse words a special device of 'actualization'.)
Expressive syntax, frequent usage of exclamatory sentences, rhetorical
questions and apostrophes constitute another important component of the
bookish style of *The End of the Old Times*. Many of these verbal means,
primarily the syntactic ones, form the special narrative devices aimed at
putting the narrator in direct contact with his reader (see above and also
C2 following).[18]

It seems to me that the analysis above has provided sufficient evidence
for our initial assumption that some of the phenomena, antithetical in
Čapek's and Vančura's individual styles, can be related to a common feature of the stylistic 'deep structure': to the abolition of the traditional
opposition between the speech levels of the narrator and the characters.
Čapek's colloquial-style narrative, in both the third-person and the first-
person forms, with its recreation of devices of oral, pre-literary story-telling,
and Vančura's archaization of the characters' speech, his use of pre-realistic
narrative devices and his creation of the bookish *Ich*-form are diverse results of the same stylistic trend.

At the same time, however, we observed one important difference between Čapek's and Vančura's solutions: Čapek arrives at a new stylistic
system by developing, to their extremes, certain trends which existed in
nineteenth-century Czech literature; in contrast, Vančura returns to some
pre-nineteenth-century narrative traditions and styles and integrates them
into the modern fictional style. This diverse historical affiliation, which has
a general import, accounts, in my opinion, for most of the basic divergences
in the 'surface structure' of Čapek's and Vančura's individual styles.

2 It was suggested in B2 that the structure and effect of fictional narrative
is substantially changed when the objective narrator is replaced by a narrator freely expressing his attitudes, commentaries and value judgements.
This fundamental feature of the 'deep structure' of modern fictional style
is reflected in the 'surface structure' of the style of both Čapek and Vančura; it is, however, again materialized in opposite ways and by opposite
devices.

Vančura creates a rhetorical narrator by activating – often to extremes –
the narrator's interpretative function; his narrator is an exposed creator
and judge of the narrated events and of the depicted characters, making
explicitly known his attitudes, value judgements and feelings. However,
this narrator, in the same way as the objective narrator, is separated from

---

18 Later on, Vančura attempted to write a cycle of *Ich*-stories based on different
speech levels. Two of them, using substandard forms of spoken Czech, were published
shortly before Vančura's death.

the world of his characters; he is not one of them, but rather is above them and above the story he tells. In contrast, Čapek activates his characters, making them participants in the narrative act itself; in other words, Čapek's characters assume the representational function. The subjective *Er*-form results from this participation: narrated events are rendered in the *Er*-form, but through the mediation of a certain character's subjectivity.

We can hardly find a better description of Vančura's rhetorical narrator than one given in the words of Spera, the narrator of *The End of the Old Times*:

5/ In any case, I don't believe in your denatured and unsalted methods of telling a story. In contradistinction to hypocrites and philistines, I assert that every story should be spiced with love and hate. It ought to give off the aroma of the pot in which it was boiled, and to be told in such a way that you may recognize the cook, as a wine-drinker recognizes the vineyard where his bottle was grown.

It is obvious that for this 'method of telling a story' the *Ich*-form is the best of all available modes. Vančura, however, makes the narrator of his *Er*-narratives no less involved. Let us deal briefly with a typical example of Vančura's rhetoric – with his short story 'The Honest Pint' ('*Dobrá míra*') from a collection entitled *Queen Dorothea's Bow* (*Luk královny Dorotky*, 1932). In this tale, Vančura's narrator unfolds the venerable drama of love, jealousy and death; at the same time, he comments on it with good humour and a sprinkling of irony. In some of his commentaries, the narrator emerges from his *Er*-anonymity and expresses his value statement in the first person:

6/ She [Isabella] was in her early thirties – oh, what a lovely age! The hips begin to round, the breasts become heavy and sag a little. I won't say that fifteen years isn't a better age than thirty odd, but at such an early age one is in no hurry, and that would not do.

The reader too is drawn into the narrative game; he becomes the addressee of the narrator's questions, appeals and doubts, especially in passages of the narrator's moralizing. Sometimes given specific traits, the reader becomes a partner in a one-sided dialogue with the narrator who tries to convince him about the correctness of his attitude:

7/ Does it give you pleasure to observe your darling in transports of music? Are you sure Beethoven has never before been played so well? Your neighbours do not share your view and say she bangs the keyboard and deafens their ears. Oh, it is indeed a difficult thing to agree on what is beautiful and what is proper. In the long run, it is possible to defend Isabella and Cyprian. Indeed, we shall defend them at your own expense, you rogues and fine ladies who all commit sin in your thoughts like a pack of goats. It is only your decrepit bodies that give you an air of continence, for you cannot fulfil even half of your dreams.

Thus both the narrator and the reader are 'activated' to overcome the alienation between the two participants of the communicative act, so typical of the 'written' culture. With respect to these features, M. Grygar appositely compared Vančura's narrator to a preacher.[19]

Let us now turn to Čapek's favourite narrative mode – the subjective *Er*-form. This mode is well known in modern fiction.[20] Its 'subjective camera' is by no means an indifferent apparatus; rather, it is the sensitive and reacting human mind. Not only the 'external' narrated events but also the interior reactions and mental processes of the mediator are expressed in narrative. It seems to me that the simultaneity of 'extrospection' and 'introspection' brings about the main effect of this technique. The following passage from Čapek's novel *Krakatit* will illustrate the point:

8/ Soon after ten o'clock the Princess herself came out, accompanied by the heir to the throne, and set out for the Japanese pavilion. Prokop suddenly felt giddy; it seemed to him that he was falling head first; he convulsively clutched at the branches, trembling all over. Nobody followed them; on the contrary, all the rest quickly left the park and gathered together in front of the castle. Probably a final conversation or something of the sort. Prokop bit his lips so as not to cry out. It took a great deal of time, perhaps an hour, perhaps five. And then the heir ran back alone, his face red and his fists clenched.

The whole scene is depicted through the medium of an 'observer' – the protagonist of the novel, Prokop. Only what was accessible to Prokop's observation is recorded. However, Prokop is not an indifferent witness; his

19 M. Grygar, *Rozbor moderní básnické epiky. Vančurův Pekař Jan Marhoul* [An Analysis of Modern Poetic Epic. Vančura's *Jan Marhoul, the Baker*], Rozpravy Československé akademie věd, Řada společenských věd, Prague, 1970, vol. i, p. 23.

20 'Possibly,' hints R. Wellek, 'Karel Čapek has learned directly or indirectly something from the masters of perspective in modern fiction – from Henry James or Joseph Conrad, or even more likely he has himself developed a method in his search for truth which remains always in perspective only.' (*Essays on Czech Literature*, The Hague, 1963, p. 58.)

strong emotional involvement in the narrated events is rendered. Let us note one characteristic detail: the duration of the conversation is not given in 'objective' time but in the 'subjective' time of Prokop's excitement.

The technique of the subjective Er-form is a prominent tool of profound psychological analysis in which modern fiction excels. Čapek's sophisticated usage of the technique, together with his elaboration of the stream-of-consciousness style, testifies to the fact that at least one group of Čapek's prose writings represents an important contribution to the development of the modern Czech psychological novel.[21] This group, of course, contains not only Er-narratives but also Ich-narratives, culminating in the first-person novel An Ordinary Life (Obyčejný život, 1934).

Čapek's and Vančura's Ich-form, the most explicit mode of the subjective narrator, was dealt with, at least in one aspect, in cl. Here I would like to make only a brief comment on one other aspect of the Ich-form in their fiction. It seems to me that in traditional fiction, Ich-narrative was a 'marked' form as distinct from the 'unmarked' Er-narrative. The Ich-form was used only in special circumstances, whereas the Er-form could be used without limitations. The special circumstances of the Ich-form were described in its motivation: usually, the Ich-narrative was expressly specified as autobiography, memoir, notes, confession, story-telling, or the like.

It should be noted that in the most important Ich-narratives of our protagonists – in Čapek's An Ordinary Life and in Vančura's The End of the Old Times – the motivation is preserved; both of them are introduced as notes (or memoirs). It seems to me, however, that Čapek and Vančura were in tune with the development of the modern Ich-form. This development can, perhaps, best be described as the transformation of a marked form into an unmarked one. In Vančura's later cycle of Ich-stories, mentioned in footnote 18, as well as in Čapek's last (and unfinished) piece of fiction, The Life and Work of the Composer Foltýn (Život a dílo skladatele Foltýna, 1939) [English translation under the title The Cheat], the traditional motivation is dropped. (As has been mentioned, Čapek's Tales from the Other Pocket also lacks the expected motivating frame.) Ich-form, once a marked mode of narrative, no longer needs fictional motivation. It is a conventionalized form of narrative in the same degree as the Er-narrative. This transformation of the Ich-form, to which both Čapek and Vančura made contributions, is, in my opinion, one of the most telling

21 This has been stressed also by E. Strohsová, although she was primarily concerned with Čapek's 'action novels', 'Román pro služky a Čapkovo směřování k epičnosti' [The Novel for Maids and Čapek's Quest toward Epic] in M. Jankovič, Z. Pešat, F. Vodička (eds.), Struktura a smysl literárního díla, Prague, 1966, p. 135.

manifestations of the general tendency of modern narrative towards explicit subjectiveness.[22]

3 It was assumed in B3 that the traditional narrative, homogeneous in its speech level and its semantic structure, was transformed into a narrative unstable both in its speech level and in its semantics. In this section of our comparative investigation, it will be demonstrated that, again, both Čapek's and Vančura's fiction share this important stylistic tendency; at the same time, this tendency is materialized in different ways.

Assigning speech-level unhomogeneity to Čapek's and Vančura's narrative may seem contradictory to what was said in C1. However, we should bear in mind that Čapek's colloquial speech level and Vančura's bookish speech level operate as the general base of their respective narratives; the means of other speech levels are interspersed within the general bases, creating, more or less frequently, contrasts and tensions.

It has to be emphasized that both the frequency and the range of speech-level discords is substantially lower with Čapek than with Vančura.[23] Moreover, Čapek's narrative is characterized primarily by motivated speech-level shifts, i.e. by shifts determined by the content (theme) or by compositional factors. Motivated shifts from the colloquial to the journalistic or scientific style are particularly frequent in Čapek's feuilleton novels, *Factory for the Absolute* and *The War with the Newts*.[24] There is, however, one important instance of unmotivated speech-level shifts in Čapek's narrative: shifts from colloquialisms to poetic images. Rather, we should describe this phenomenon as the rise of poetic images from the colloquial speech-level base. Colloquialisms and poetic figures are so intimately interwoven in Čapek's narrative that its style could be best designated as *colloquial poeticalness*.[25]

---

22 We could hardly find a better example of the conventionalized character of *Ich*-form narrative in contemporary Czech fiction than the story *Closely Watched Trains* (*Ostře sledované vlaky*, 1965) by B. Hrabal. Here, the narrator and protagonist of the story not only dies at the end, but even describes his own death.

23 Extremely bookish speech level, represented by the 'sacral style', is used by Čapek mostly for parody – cf. W. Schamschula, 'Der sakrale Stil und seine Funktion im Werk Karel Čapeks' in M. Braun, E. Koschmieder, I. Mahnken (eds.), *Slawistische Studien zum V. Internationalen Slawistenkongress in Sofia 1963*, Göttingen, 1963, pp. 445–55.

24 Cf. this statement about *Factory for the Absolute*: 'The novel is a brilliant pastiche of the most diverse kinds of writings: newspaper articles, memoirs, scholarly works, manifestos, etc.' (W. Harkins, *Karel Čapek*, New York – London, 1962, p. 95.) See also Harkins' explanation of the speech-level shifts in *Hordubal* ('Imagery in Karel Čapek's *Hordubal*', PMLA, LXXV (1960), p. 617).

25 W. Harkins described in detail the rise of a group of poetic images in *Hordubal* from the everyday 'agricultural' vocabulary (in the article quoted in footnote 24).

In this respect, Čapek is at his best in minor genres, travel sketches, tales for children, feuilletons, etc. It is the colloquial poeticalness which accounts to a high degree for the charm and the popularity of these texts. Let us give some examples here from *Letters from England* (*Anglické listy*, 1924):

9/ The London streets are just a gulley through which life flows to get quickly home.

Only the Sheep, the Cows and the Horses ruminate deliberately and without haste on the beauties of nature.

Čapek's technique is based on an unusual use of colloquial expressions and idioms; he puts them into contexts wherein they cannot be used in common speech. In such a way, a conspicuous semantic shift occurs; the colloquial speech level of the context, however, is preserved: *life ... getting home, the sheep ... ruminating ... on the beauties of nature.* Quite often, this device is 'laid bare', when the colloquial expression or idiom is combined with a string of expressions, some of which are semantically adequate, others inadequate:

10/ The Highlanders stand at attention, behind them the castle of the Scottish kings, and still farther behind them, the whole blood-stained and dreadful history of this land.

Only an English lawn and an English gentleman are shaved every day.

In Čapek's style, the discovery of poetry behind everyday colloquial speech is parallel to the discovery of the universe behind familiar places, or to the discovery of personal plurality behind the mask of an 'ordinary life'. I feel that this extraction of poetry and eternity from things and words that are inconspicuous, faded, ephemeral and time-worn is more than a feature of Karel Čapek's style; it is a specific quality of modern Czech literature.

In Vančura's narrative, speech level and semantic incongruencies are not only more frequent, but also more conspicuous than those described in Čapek's style. Vančura's narrative tends to extremes, combining, on the one hand, biblical archaisms and, on the other, vulgar and coarse words.[26]

26 In *Pekař Jan Marhoul*, the speech-level span of narrative ranges from 'the calm and idyllic narrative mode of a fairy-tale' to 'the excited, pathetic declamation' (Grygar, p. 211; see footnote 16).

Within a short context, sharp stylistic and semantic clashes are condensed because of unconventional, surprising word combinations:

11/ As Hora drank, the picture and the brandy gradually waned until the empty tumbler enclosed the drunkard's nose like the gardener's hotcap covers the asparagus sprout.

The church tower loomed up above the town stupidly and brazenly, as though the heights of the sky at which it pointed with its needle-like steeple were not uninhabited, but rather as if something was going on way up there. In the ropes of night the stars flickered too ominously for them to be consoling, and along the bottom of the town, the drunken sots crawled off to their taverns.

Death. That is the word, that is the sound, that is the rustling, that is the butterfly which darts from light to light and beats its wings.

'Drunkard's nose' compared with 'asparagus sprout', church towers looming up 'stupidly and brazenly', the juxtaposition of 'stars' and 'drunken sots', death presented as a 'butterfly', these are semantic contrasts and shifts typical of Vančura. Introducing them in high frequency into his texts together with the features described in C1 and C2, Vančura creates a new, original prose style, breaking away from the traditions of prosaic language and approaching, instead, the principles of poetic language.

According to Coleridge, let us recall, good prose is characterized by the use of 'proper words in proper places'; this 'prosaic principle' was implemented in Czech nineteenth-century realistic fiction with amazing consistency. And Coleridge's 'poetic principle' – 'the most proper words in their proper places' – is, as a matter of fact, an extreme case of the 'prosaic principle'. Twentieth-century avant-garde literature reversed Coleridge's hierarchy and, at the same time, gave a new content to the 'poetic principle'. The new poetic principle, described in various terms by the critics ('making strange', 'laying bare', 'actualization', 'focus on the verbal sign itself', 'poetic deviation', etc.), requires 'improper words in their improper places' in order to destroy the conventional relationship between the verbal sign and its referent. Modern poetry breaks away from the conventions of the referential (communicative) language and creates its own semantics, based on specific 'violations' of the conventional semantic rules.

Avant-garde Czech prose fiction adopts the new 'poetic principle'.[27] It is no longer interested in creating a 'mock reality' by means of a referential report, but rather in creating a poetic world, which, not unlike the world of modern painting, is autonomous in its qualities, shapes and colours.

It seems to me that the transformation of the traditional fictional style into its antithesis in modern fiction was initiated by the new aesthetic ideal of prose fiction. All the narrative devices of a referential report had to be abolished. Instead, specific *story-telling* devices and means of poetic representation had to be introduced (or re-introduced) into fictional style. In this way, modern prose fiction, preserving its specificity, was enabled to join avant-garde poetry (and other arts) in striving for a new aesthetic ideal.

In this essay, we have attempted to illustrate that the general stylistic trend of modern prose fiction allows for a variety of individual manifestations. Karel Čapek and Vladislav Vančura, although typifying the same general trend of modern 'poetic prose', represent, at the same time, highly different personalities and, we may say, different traditions in modern Czech literature.

27 There has been no doubt about Vančura's close relationship to the Czech avant-garde; about the connection of Čapek's prose fiction (and of his theory of fiction) with avant-garde ideals, see J. Opelík, 'Obyčejný život čili Deukalion' [An Ordinary Life, or Deukalion] in *Struktura a smysl literárního díla*, Prague, 1966, p. 151f.

5

'Narrative symposium' in Milan Kundera's *The Joke*

In the history of fiction, a system of narrative modes has been created, offering alternative ways of presenting narrated events. Moreover, whenever a 'personalized' narrator is implied by the narrative mode (such is the case, primarily, with the *Ich*-form narratives and the subjective *Er*-form), the narrated events can be presented in various subjective perspectives ('points of view'). Let us call the combination of a narrative mode with a particular perspective *narrative form*. Narrative forms can be employed in two different ways: Either the whole text of a short story or a novel is homogeneous, i.e. it is narrated in one and the same narrative form; or the text is heterogeneous, i.e. different portions of the text are presented in different narrative modes and/or perspectives. A heterogeneous text consists of formally differentiated *narrative segments*.

The transition from one narrative segment to another can be motivated by the *story-telling situation* depicted in the context. The story-telling situation is a set of motifs expressing the temporal, spatial and other circumstances of the act of narrating; it can be, but need not be, a part of the narrator's situation (defined here, p. 16).[1] Motivated shifts are typical for such narrative forms as short story within a novel,[2] the novel with a frame, the epistolary novel, most short story cycles and fictional diaries, etc. For

1 Todorov's brilliant analysis revealed a complete fusion of the story-telling and the narrator's situations in the *Thousand and One Nights* (T. Todorov, 'Les hommes-récits', Appendix to *Grammaire du Décaméron*, The Hague – Paris, 1969).

2 Cf. R. Wellek, A. Warren, *The Theory of Literature*, 2nd edition, New York, 1956, p. 211.

modern prose fiction, however, unmotivated shifts of narrative segments are quite typical. Narrative modes and narrative perspectives alternate without any depiction of the story-telling situation. This free, unmotivated manipulation of various narrative modes and perspectives is made possible by the historical development of modern fiction which has led to the complete conventionalization of all narrative modes (cf. here, pp. 107–8).

A *multiperspective novel*, a novel of shifting 'points of view', is the result of the alternation of narrative forms. Instead of a stable and constant perspective associated with one organizing agent, the multiperspective novel presents the narrated events from various angles, in an objective as well as subjective rendering, from the 'outside', and from the 'inside', through the minds of various characters. Narrated events in this narrative structure are projected into a multidimensional universe and thus acquire multiple meanings and interpretations.

Some critics thought of the multiperspective technique as a manifestation of a crisis in the modern novel; it has been blamed for the destruction of the consistent semantic attitude and of the fixed system of values associated with the homogeneous narrative. Shifts and alterations of narrative forms, however, are well known in the history of fiction; they were quite common in romantic fiction.[3] Later on, a preference for the homogeneous narrative became established in the realistic schools of fiction. At the same time, however, as the subjective *Er*-form developed, the technique of shifting perspectives in the framework of the *Er*-form was tried out and became commonplace in twentieth-century fiction (cf. here, pp. 53–5). In the light of these historical facts, the technique of shifting narrative forms can be regarded as a well-established device of fiction. It arises from a consistent and most effective deployment of the fundamental structural opposition in fiction, that between the narrator and the narrated events; it is, to use the terminology of the Prague school, the systematic actualization ('foregrounding') of the narrator.

Generally speaking, the multiperspective technique may be used in either of two opposite ways:

1 The same (or rather, approximately the same) set of narrated events is repeated two or more times in two or more different narrative forms. We get, as it were, a cycle of narratives different in their narrative mode and/

3 See, for example, the narrative structure of M.J. Lermontov's *The Hero of Our Time*. J. Mersereau (*Mikhail Lermontov*, Carbondale, Ill., 1962, pp. 75–80) described the alternation of narrators in Lermontov's novel and pointed out that it served an essential function – a gradual 'approximation' of the characterization of the main hero (Pečorin).

or perspective, but equivalent, approximately, in their content (theme). Let us call this variant of the multiperspective technique *the cyclic structure*. A general characterization of the technique was given by Jan Muka-řovský in his description of the narrative pattern of Karel Čapek's *Hordubal*: 'We see the course of events in three different illuminations: now, as it was observed by Hordubal himself, a taciturn and passive man (we are, as it were, transferred into his place, we do not perceive the facts themselves, but Hordubal's thoughts about the facts); now, as it is seen and judged by policemen investigating the murder and, ultimately, how it appears in the light of the trial.'[4]

2 Different sets of narrated events are rendered in different narrative modes and/or perspectives. In other words, the action of the short story or novel is narrated only once, but various segments of the action are expressed in various narrative forms. Let us call this variant of the multiperspective technique *the linear structure*. Marie Pujmanová's short novel *The Premonition* (*Předtucha*, 1942) is an example of this structure. Here, segments of action, presented from different perspectives in the subjective *Er*-form, are arranged in chronological order. In the novel *Follow the Green Light* (*Jdi za zeleným světlem*, 1956) by Edvard Valenta, linear structure is associated with a specific organization of the fictional time: the 'contemporary' action is narrated in the *Er*-form, whereas the 'prehistory' is rendered in the *Ich*-form. Chapters of the *Er*-form and *intermezzi* of the *Ich*-form alternate in a regular rhythm, both arranged chronologically. Thus, the time of the *Er*-form action and the time of the *Ich*-form action gradually merge.

This general account of the multiperspective technique should provide a suitable framework for discussing a very interesting and highly original use of the technique in Milan Kundera's novel *The Joke* (*Žert*, 1967).[5] A follower of the tradition of the multiperspective novel in modern Czech fiction, Kundera made a substantial contribution to the development of its devices and functions.

The story of *The Joke* is conveyed by four *Ich*-narrators. The chief narrator, Ludvík Jahn, is the main protagonist of the novel. Three secondary

4 J. Mukařovský, *Kapitoly z české poetiky*, Prague, 1948, vol. II, p. 338. T. Todorov described the cyclic structure in the epistolary novel: 'Les romans par lettres du xviiie siècle utilisaient couramment cette technique ... qui consiste à raconter la même histoire plusieurs fois mais vue par des personnages différents.' ('Les catégories du récit littéraire', *Communications*, viii (1966), p. 143.)

5 The second edition of the novel was published in Prague in 1968. An English translation (with serious omissions) was published in New York in 1969. (Our quotations refer to the first Czech edition).

narrators, Helena, Jaroslav, and Kostka, all have (or had) a close relationship to Ludvík: Helena as his 'victim', Jaroslav as his old classmate, Kostka as his friend and ideological antagonist.

Although the stories of all secondary narrators are outlined in the novel, the action of *The Joke* centres on the story of Ludvík. Coming from a small town in southern Moravia, he becomes a political activist during his university days in Prague (in the early 1950s). However, a political joke he makes casually is taken seriously; his former comrade Zemánek is instrumental in Ludvík's expulsion from the party and from the university. Consequently, Ludvík is drafted into a penal battalion to serve in the mines of Ostrava; he even spends several years in prison. In Ostrava, he experiences a tragic love affair with Lucie. Later, he is 'rehabilitated', but never gives up his plan for revenge on Zemánek. He hopes to carry out this revenge by seducing Zemánek's wife, Helena, during a visit to his Moravian hometown. However, this revenge turns into an absurd joke: Ludvík learns that Zemánek himself wants to get rid of Helena.

Ludvík's story is rendered in seven chapters, with a strict distribution of narrators: odd chapters (the first, the third and the fifth) are assigned to Ludvík, even chapters to the other participants of the narrative symposium (the second, to Helena; the fourth, to Jaroslav; the sixth, to Kostka). The final, seventh chapter is divided into shorter narrative segments rendered alternatively by three narrators, active participants in the final Moravian episode (Ludvík, Helena, Jaroslav). Ludvík again is assigned the odd segments (from one to nineteen), Helena and Jaroslav share the even segments (Helena: four, fourteen, sixteen; Jaroslav: all the others).[6]

The fundamental problem of the narrative structure of *The Joke* consists in the selection of the narrators. Why were these characters and not any of the others entrusted with the function of narrating? The selection of narrators was not fortuitous but determined, I believe, by the structure and type of Kundera's novel. Typologically, *The Joke* can be designated an *ideological novel* (novel of ideas), i.e. a novel dominated in its structure by the plane of ideas.[7] The narrators of *The Joke* are representatives of

6 An interesting count was made by M. Blahynka: If we take the length of Helena's narrative monologue as a unit, then Kostka's narrative measures approximately two units, Jaroslav's – three units, Ludvík's – twelve units (M. Blahynka, 'M. Kundera prozaik' [M. Kundera as Prosaist], *Plamen*, no. 1 (1967), p. 50).

7 The term 'ideological novel' was used by Engel'gardt to describe Dostoyevsky's novels. The dominant component of the structure of Dostoyevsky's novels is, according to Engel'gardt, 'a central idea', determining the peculiar traits of his characters (B.M. Engel'gardt, 'Ideologičeskij roman Dostojevskogo' [Dostoyevsky's Ideological Novel]

various systems of 'false' ideologies-myths; their narrative monologues are *authentic accounts of the social conditions and of the individual directions of the destruction of myths.*[8]

The typological character of Kundera's novel determines the selection of narrators not only in a positive but also in a negative sense, i.e. by eliminating certain potential candidates. Two important agents in Ludvík's story – his 'enemy' Zemánek and his love Lucie – are not assigned the function of narrator. Their contributions to the narrative symposium are not required because they have nothing to say about the destruction of myths. Zemánek is an opportunist who simply exchanges an old myth for a new one (the myth of the new generation); he adjusts his ideology comfortably to changes of ideological fashion and, therefore, is unable to live and to report the tragedy of a myth being destroyed. Lucie's story, on the contrary, is tragic, but her tragedy is not ideological; it is a personal, intimate tragedy of 'defilement'.

Lucie's absence from the narrative symposium can be related also to a factor of the plot structure of the novel. In the plot construction of *The Joke*, Lucie assumes the role of 'mystery'. She is the 'goddess of escape' (Ludvík), both by her name, and by her role in Ludvík's personal tragedy. She is a romantic character with a mysterious past and ambiguous motivations. It is obvious that Lucie's own narration, her self-revelation, would destroy the atmosphere of romantic mystery surrounding her personality and actions.[9] Therefore, Lucie's aspect of the story is not rendered directly, but through the mediation of Kostka who is, as will be shown later, a rather 'unreliable' narrator; in this mediation, the romantic savour of Lucie's fate and of her motivations is not dispersed, but rather reinforced.

---

in A.S. Dolinin (ed.), *Dostojevskij. Statji i materialy*, Leningrad, 1925, vol. II, p. 86). It is interesting to note that M. Bachtin connected Dostoyevsky's ideological novel with the tradition of the 'Menippean satire' (*Problemy poetiki Dostojevskogo* [Problems of Dostoyevsky's Poetics], Moscow, 1963, pp. 150–62). In Northrop Frye's typology, the 'ideological novel' is called *anatomy*. In anatomy, 'the dramatic interest is in a conflict of ideas rather than of characters' (*Anatomy of Criticism*, 8th ed., New York, 1969, p. 310). Independent of Bachtin, Frye also pointed to the importance of the 'Menippean satire' for the prehistory of this narrative type.

8 Cf. the following statement by M. Pohorský: 'The exposing of the false consciousness of all four narrators is the essential principle of Kundera's novel.' (M. Pohorský, 'Komika Kunderova Žertu' [The Comic Aspects of Kundera's *The Joke*], *Česká literatura*, XVII (1969), p. 340.)

9 It is true that Lucie's mystery could be preserved even in her self-revelation; however, this could be achieved only at the cost of a rather cheap narrative trick (cf. Barthes's criticism of two novels of Agatha Christie which 'ne maintient l'enigme qu'en trichant sur la personne de la narration' ('Introduction à l'analyse structurale des récits', *Communications*, VIII (1966), p. 20).

In order to describe the narrative structure of *The Joke* in more detail, let us now turn to the investigation of the performances of the particular narrators, to the organization and style of their narrative monologues. It seems to me that the specific features of the particular narrative monologues reflect various stages of the myth-destroying process which the narrators have reached. Specifically, the structure and texture of the narrative monologue depends on the balance of two functions of narrator, namely the *representational* and the *interpretative* function. We assume that the balance of representation and interpretation, different in the particular narrative monologues of *The Joke*, reflects the narrator's stage in the myth-destroying process.

In Helena's narrative, interpretation dominates over representation. The destruction of Helena's myth occurs solely under external pressures; she herself is incapable of a critical rejection of her myth and its phraseology. Helena's myth remains naive from the beginning to the end. Her faked 'suicide' is a grotesque symbol of the perseverance of a naive myth. Helena's naiveté is also reflected in the style of her narrative. This style is very close to what is called 'stream-of-consciousness style', an uncontrolled, unorganized, spontaneous flow of freely associated motifs, trite phrases and expressions:

1/ We gave hundreds of performances and shows, sang Soviet songs, our new songs and, of course, folk-songs, we liked singing them best, I fell so much in love with Moravian songs that, though I am from Pilsen, I used to think of myself as Moravian and they became the theme of my life ...

And afterwards we sat in a little inn at Zbraslav, ate bread and sausage, everything was so plain and ordinary, the grumpy inn-keeper, the stained tablecloth, and yet it was a lovely adventure.

Kostka's evangelical myth is just the opposite of Helena's naive ideology. In his narrative performance, however, Kostka is very close to Helena. Interpretation clearly dominates over representation in his narrative. Destruction of Kostka's refractory myth is not completed; it is carried only to the stage of unsolvable dilemmas. Kostka continues to use the terms and phraseology of his impaired myth to interpret his own story as well as the stories of the other protagonists. Because of the dominance of interpretation over representation in Kostka's narrative, Kostka seems to be the least reliable narrator of the symposium. This unreliability is especially revealed in his rendering of Lucie's story. In order to satisfy an *a priori* interpretation, Lucie's affair with Ludvík must be presented as another case of 'defilement'; Kostka himself then can assume the prescribed role of Lucie's saviour.

The phraseology of Kostka's evangelical myth comprises the fundamental, distinctive stratum of his narrative style. Quotations and paraphrases of New Testament locutions figure as the most conspicuous device in that stratum. Moreover, Kostka's narrative style is saturated with a recurrent rhetoric, addressed to his ever-present ideological antagonist Ludvík:

2/ You once stated that socialism grew from the stem of European rationalism and skepticism, a stem which was non-religious and anti-religious, and that it is otherwise unthinkable. Do you seriously maintain that it is impossible to build a socialist society without faith in the supremacy of matter? Do you really think that men who believe in God are incapable of nationalizing factories?

Again it is typical of Kostka's rhetoric that it is aimed in the wrong direction and becomes grotesque. Quite in the spirit of the great grotesque battles of the novelistic tradition, Kostka's impaired myth falls upon Ludvík's myth which, in the meantime, Ludvík himself has already repudiated.

Whereas in Kostka's narrative the subjective interpretation adjusts the introduced motifs to its own ends, Jaroslav's monologue is built on a parallelism of representation and interpretation. It presents narrated events on two parallel and disjointed levels, that of folkloristic myth and that of 'everyday life'. Jaroslav's archaic myth interprets the motifs of his narrative in the terms, symbolism and phraseology of folk poetry. At the same time, however, the narrator himself is aware of the inadequacy of such an interpretation; Jaroslav comes to regard his myth as 'dreaming' and 'fantasy'. Nevertheless, he still is not ready to give up trying 'to live in two worlds at the same time'. For others, however, Jaroslav's folkloristic interpretations are almost ridiculous; they create shadows of the narrated events which the participants of these events refuse to accept as authentic.

Jaroslav's narrative monologue is very special in that it gives a systematic, one might almost say, scientific account of his myth and its transformations. This component of the interpretative function (interpretation of the interpretation) explains the density of professional language drawn from history and musical theory in Jaroslav's narrative style:

3/ The Czech language retreated from the towns to the countryside and became the exclusive property of the illiterate. Among them, however, it never ceased creating its own culture – a humble culture, completely hidden from the eyes of Europe. A culture of songs, fairy-tales, ancient rites and customs, proverbs and sayings.

Jaroslav's expert treatise on Moravian folklore[10] represents one extreme pole of the stylistic variety of *The Joke*, the other one being represented by the loose and spontaneous style of Helena's monologue.

Jaroslav's myth is substantiated in terms of rational arguments. On the other hand, its destruction is brought about in the most extreme and cruel manner. In the last chapter of the novel (not only in Jaroslav's but also in Ludvík's rendering), the folkloristic myth is totally defiled. Surprisingly, however, in the moment of deepest humiliation, it experiences a glorious, although short-lived resurrection. The 'abandoned' folkloristic myth flashes for awhile 'with an irresistible ultimate beauty' and in this beauty it becomes for Ludvík the symbol of his home, finally re-discovered. This harmonic chord seems for awhile to be the conclusion of Ludvík's cacophonous life story. But it is not allowed to peter out; it is interrupted suddenly by Jaroslav's fall. In a narrative structure which is based on the destruction of myths, the resurrection of a myth cannot be used as the dénouement.

It is Ludvík who offers the most important contribution to the narrative symposium of *The Joke*. His monologue dominates the narrative structure of the novel not only because it introduces the most important episodes of the action, but also because it presents the most profound and most conscious destruction of a myth. Mythological interpretation is replaced by critical analysis; a perfect harmony between the narrator's representational 'responsibility' and his interpretative function is thus achieved. This state of harmony is facilitated by two essential features of Ludvík's story. First, in no other story is the destruction of myth so closely connected with personal tragedy. Second, Ludvík's character shows from the very beginning both a *Lust zum Fabulieren* and an inclination to self-analysis, to critical evaluation of one's own deeds and words. Ludvík excels in the merciless 'tearing away of veils'.

It is, therefore, not surprising that Ludvík is assigned the role of destroying not only his own myth but also of contributing substantially to the destruction of other characters' myths. Describing his first meeting with Helena, Ludvík reports his deep aversion to her hackneyed and time-serving phraseology. Ludvík exposes the hypocrisy of Jaroslav's actualization of folklore in his brief description of Jaroslav's wedding. For Kostka,

10 In the English translation, the most substantial part of this treatise is, unfortunately, omitted.

'God's mason', he reserves a slight irony. He treats the anti-myth of the younger generation with much more biting irony.

In this connection, I would like to mention specifically Ludvík's depiction of the ceremony of 'the welcoming of new citizens into life' (chapter v). Here we find a meticulous application of the device of 'making strange',[11] an application which in its consistency and sophistication is unique in Czech literature. 'Tearing away of veils' is accomplished here solely by a literary device, by the depiction of the scene from a special angle, from the viewpoint of a stranger who does not understand what is going on. This angle renders all actions, words and emotions void, meaningless and disconnected. Only after this absurd depiction is the 'meaning' of the ceremony revealed (in Ludvík's conversation with the official who performed the ceremony).

Ludvík's passion for the 'tearing away of veils' is reflected in his narrative style through relentless enumeration of dreary or ugly details which, appearing sometimes in parentheses, distort every picture:

4/ We left the hospital and soon arrived at a new housing project whose buildings loomed crookedly one after another from the unlevelled dusty site (grassless, unpaved, streetless) and made a drab setting at the edge of the town where it bordered the empty spaces of far-stretching fields. We entered a door, climbed the narrow stairway (the elevator was not working) and did not stop until the third floor.

It would be a great mistake, however, to call Ludvík's narrative style 'naturalistic'. A more detailed investigation of his monologue would reveal a complex, multilayered texture, where detailed descriptiveness with a bias for ugly details represents only one extreme pole; it is balanced by uninhibited poetic language expressed in rhythmical syntax and in symbolic imagery:

5/ From that evening on, everything changed in me; I was once again inhabited; I ceased being that deplorable vacancy where languor, reproaches, complaints lay flung about (like rubbish in a looted room); suddenly, the room of my

---

11 A classic characterization of the device of 'making strange' (*ostranenije*) in Tolstoy's fiction was given by V. Šklovskij in his *O teorii prozy* [On the Theory of Prose], Moscow, 1925 (see esp. the essay 'Iskusstvo kak prijem' [Art as Device], English translation in L. Lemon, M. J. Reis (eds.), *Russian Formalist Criticism*, Lincoln, Nebraska, 1965).

heart had been tidied up and someone was living there. The clock that had hung on its wall for months with motionless hands all at once began to tick.

The opposite poles of everyday speech and subtle poetic language, which have been described in Karel Čapek's style (cf. pp. 108–9), clearly emerge in Ludvík's narrative monologue. Moreover, this monologue is a good illustration of the stylistic complexity and versatility which is characteristic of many *Ich*-narrators in contemporary Czech fiction. Besides the type of *Ich*-narrator whose style is based on a certain homogeneous speech level, modern fiction presents numerous examples of *versatile Ich-narrators* who are characterized by speech-level shifts and semantic contrasts. This stylistic versatility seems to be an appropriate expression of the complex experiences and of the constantly changing attitudes associated with the literary image of modern man.[12]

Up to now we have concentrated on the study of correlations between the narrative and the ideological structure of *The Joke*. The study of these correlations revealed that the form of narrative symposium used in the novel is not mere fashionable whimsy; rather it is a device by which is realized multiple destruction and self-destruction of myths which are, one might say, the real protagonists of this ideological novel. However, the correlations just described represent only one of the functions of the narrative symposium of *The Joke*; other functions can be revealed when studying *correlations between the narrative structure and the structure of fictional time*. The second part of this essay is devoted to the study of this important aspect of Kundera's novel.

The basic feature of fictional time in *The Joke* is quite typical for modern fiction: the proper chronology of events is done away with and replaced by achronological confrontations and clashes of narrated events occurring on different time-planes, in different time-periods. The action of *The Joke* is concentrated in two time-periods. The first period, Ludvík's expulsion from the university and his military service in the mines of Ostrava, will be called *the Ostrava episode*; the second, Ludvík's visit to his hometown in southern Moravia (with the aim of executing his long prepared 're-venge'), will be called *the Moravian episode*. Two secondary time-periods

---

12 Another example of the versatile *Ich*-narrator in contemporary Czech literature (a short novel by A. Lustig) was described in L. Doležel, J. Kuchař (eds.), *Knížka o jazyce a stylu soudobé české literatury* [A Book on the Language and Style of Contemporary Czech Literature], Prague, 1961, p. 23. J. Škvorecký's *The Cowards* (*Zbabělci*, 1958) is an excellent prototype of this narrative style in contemporary Czech fiction.

alternate with the periods of the main action: *the prehistory*, comprising
the sequence of events of Ludvík's childhood and studies in Prague preceding the Ostrava episode, and *the intermezzo*, i.e. the sequence of
events of the time-period between the Ostrava and the Moravian episodes.
In a schematic outline, the chronology of the action in *The Joke* can be
represented as follows:

prehistory	OSTRAVA EPISODE	*intermezzo*	MORAVIAN EPISODE

The chronological action is transformed into the achronolgical structure
of the plot by adopting the time of the Moravian episode as the narrated
present; all the other time-periods of the action are then automatically
transposed into the narrated past. This temporal perspective is materialized by making the time of all the narrative acts (performances) identical
(synchronous) with the time of the Moravian episode. All narrators contributing to the narrative symposium deliver their narratives at the time
the events of the Moravian episode occur. In other words, the time of narrating is identical with the narrated time of the Moravian episode. By this
arrangement, the unexpected, grotesque dénouement of the Moravian episode can be presented as an immediate experience, captured in its *status
nascenti*; at the same time, a solid distance from the narrated events of the
mythical past is established.

The Moravian episode takes up three days, reconstructable as a Friday,
Saturday and Sunday. The time of particular narrative acts is indicated by
explicit references which date the acts to the established framework of
narrated time. On the basis of these references, we can date each narrative
performance:

Friday:　Ludvík's narrative (chapter i); Helena's narrative (chapter ii);
　　　　　Ludvík's narrative (chapter iii); Jaroslav's narrative (chapter
　　　　　iv)
Saturday: Ludvík's narrative (chapter v)
Sunday:　Kostka's narrative (chapter vi); Ludvík's, Helena's and Jaro-
　　　　　slav's narratives (chapter vii)[13]

13 The complexity of the time-structure in *The Joke* gave rise, apparently, to a minor
mistake in dating, occurring at the beginning of Kostka's narrative. Kostka gives the
date of his first meeting with Ludvík as 'yesterday', i.e. on Saturday; as a matter of fact,
the meeting occurred 'the day before yesterday' (on Friday). This is confirmed by the
correct dating of a telephone conversation with Ludvík, following the first meeting
('the day before yesterday'), as well as by the dating of the second meeting ('yesterday'). The dating of the first meeting is also unequivocally given in Ludvík's narrative
in chapter i.

It is quite obvious that the temporal distance between the time of narrating and the narrated time of the Moravian episode is negligible (or even nil in chapter vii).

The temporal proximity of all narrative performances allows for a homomorphic organization of the narrated time in all the narratives (with the exception of chapter vii which represents a special component both in the narrative and in the temporal structure of the novel). All narratives begin in the narrated present (i.e. in the time of the Moravian episode) and then return, using the device of flashback or reminiscence, to various periods of the narrated past. After having travelled a more or less complicated loop into the past, the narratives return to the present again.

There is no need here to follow in detail the time-pattern of the particular narratives and to describe the shifts from one time-period to another. Let us just note that, with a few exceptions, the narratives do not overlap. Among the exceptions, the most important is the double exposition of the climax of the Ostrava episode (the catastrophe of Ludvík's love for Lucie); two parallel depictions of this scene are offered, first in Ludvík's detailed account, the second time in Kostka's mediating of Lucie's account.[14] Besides this overlapping, there are several instances where two of the narrative monologues intersect; this occurs, usually, in scenes of minor importance (from the viewpoint of the development of the action), as, for example, in the scene of Jaroslav's wedding (intersection of Jaroslav's and Ludvík's narratives).

The interpretation of the overlapping and the intersections is crucial for our decision about the overall pattern of Kundera's multiperspective novel. In my opinion, these double exposures are not of such importance as to give us two parallel depictions of the action from two different points of view. Therefore, I do not hesitate to call the overall pattern of *The Joke* a *linear* structure. Moreover, the occasional overlapping and intersections possess, in my opinion, a different function in *The Joke*, a function which can be described on the level of the narrative structure: they show the limits of credibility, the 'reliability' of particular narrators.[15] In keeping

---

14 In this connection we could, perhaps, explain why Kostka's narrative is dated Sunday. In my opinion, there are two reasons for this arrangement: first, Kostka's absence from the Sunday narrative symposium (in chapter vii); second, and more importantly, the fact that by this arrangement a dramatic confrontation of the dénouement of the Ostrava episode with the dénouement of Ludvík's affair with Helena was made possible: Ludvík learns the reasons for his failure with Lucie immediately after the grotesque failure of his attempt at 'revenge'.

15 This was already briefly suggested by Pohorský (p. 339): 'The voices of the particular narrators proceed in such a way that they meet at certain points and thus test

with the dominance of the ideological plane in the novel's structure, the degree of the narrator's reliability is in direct proportion to the degree of the destruction of his myth. Thus Ludvík emerges as the most reliable narrator and, therefore, his representation is used to suggest the degree of unreliability of the other narrators. This holds true especially about Kostka who explicitly reveals his unreliability by the way he renders the 'overlapping' scene of the Ostrava episode.

From this particular aspect, the intricate correlations among the ideological, narrative and temporal structure of *The Joke* emerge quite distinctly. In the framework of these correlations, another important feature of the narrative symposium can also be explained, namely the assignment of particular segments of the action to particular narrators. Ludvík, who is the main hero of the myth-destroying process, is also the chief participant in the narrative symposium. His principal role is based not only on quantitative facts (see footnote 6), but particularly on qualitative aspects: he is assigned the rendering of the crucial events of the two main time-periods of the action (the Ostrava and the Moravian episodes). The contributions of the other narrators to the rendering of Ludvík's life story are comparatively minor. Helena tells about her first meetings with Ludvík (events of the *intermezzo*). Jaroslav describes some events of the prehistory (Ludvík's childhood and student years) and some rather fragmentary events of the *intermezzo*. Kostka recounts a meeting with Ludvík in the period of the prehistory and one in the time of the *intermezzo*. His main contribution consists, as already mentioned, in his mediating of Lucie's account of the Ostrava episode; the relevance of this mediation for the reconstruction of Ludvík's story is, however, undermined by Kostka's narrative unreliability. On the whole, if we limit ourselves to Ludvík's story, the linear character of the time-structure of *The Joke* seems to be violated only occasionally.

There is no need to go into an investigation of the time-structure of other protagonists' stories, as they are rendered in their own or in Ludvík's narratives. Except for a few momentary intersections, the narratives are arranged in a linear structure.

Our analysis of the time-structure of *The Joke* would be incomplete, however, if we did not deal with the special status of the last, the seventh, chapter. From the viewpoint of the action, this chapter is distinguished by the fact that it treats events of one time-period only, those of the Moravian

---

each other, correct, evaluate or discredit each other.' Our statement about the linearity of the time-structure in *The Joke* is in disagreement with Blahynka's assertion that 'almost everything is narrated twice (by Ludvík and by one of the others)'. (Blahynka, p. 52.)

episode. Moreover, the narrated events are arranged chronologically. This simplicity of the time-structure is counterbalanced by the extraordinary complexity of the narrative structure. As already pointed out, the action of chapter VII is rendered by three narrators in turn, Ludvík, Jaroslav and Helena. Narrative segments of this symposium are very different in length, from two short paragraphs to thirteen pages (in the Czech original). The narrative segments of chapter VII form a continuous, linear time-structure, without overlapping and without significant gaps.

Various interpretations of this special time and narrative structure of the last chapter of *The Joke* will certainly be offered. In my opinion, the function of this structure is purely rhythmical: an irregular, but generally rapid pattern of alternating narrative monologues is played off against the slow progress and the monotonous repetition of the leitmotif of the chapter – the ancient folkloristic ritual of the 'Ride of the Kings'. These contrasting progressions create a complex rhythmic pattern which provides an appropriate background for the grotesque culmination of Ludvík's story.

Our investigation into the problems of the narrator in Kundera's novel *The Joke* has led us to the core of the novel's artistic structure. It has revealed the ingenious network which mutually links all the principal structural components: the idea, the characters, the action, the time, the narrative form. Study of the narrator cuts across the traditional categories of form and content and gives us a rare opportunity to view the literary structure in its entirety. At the same time, we can observe how the structural network leans in a specific direction by the impact of the dominant structural component, the plane of ideas. In a period governed by collective ideologies, Kundera uses the type of the ideological novel and the form of a collective narrative symposium to ensure the best balance between the aesthetic message and the immanent structure of his novel. Following the narrative symposium of *The Joke*, we travel the peripatetic road leading from the dehumanized mythological past through the tumultuous present of myth-destruction toward a distant, but well-defined ideal of humanity.

APPENDIX: EXAMPLES IN CZECH

1 / Represented discourse in modern Czech narrative prose

EDITIONS QUOTED

ČF K. Čapek, *První parta*, Praha, 1937 (in English, London, 1939)
ČH K. Čapek, *Hordubal*, Praha, 1958 (in English, London, 1934)
ČK K. Čapek, *Krakatit*, Praha, 1939 (in English, New York, 1925)
OC J. Otčenášek, *Občan Brych*, Praha, 1956
ON I. Olbracht, *Nikola Šuhaj loupežník*, Praha, 1953 (Spisy, sv. 7)
PF M. Pujmanová, *Hra s ohněm*, Praha, 1948
PL M. Pujmanová, *Život proti smrti*, Praha, 1953
PP M. Pujmanová, *Lidé na křižovatce*, Praha, 1937
PPr M. Pujmanová, *Předtucha*, Praha, 1942
VF E. Valenta, *Jdi za zeleným světlem*, Praha, 1956

1/ 'Já se přijela podívat, Jene, jak se dnes veselíš,' přívětivě oslovila kněžna svého štolbu.
'U mé rodiny a s několika dobrými přáteli vždy dobře, Osvícenosti,' odpověděl pan Prošek. – 'Kdo je u tebe?' – 'Sousedé moji, mlynář se svou rodinou a rýznburský myslivec.' – 'Nenechej se mnou zdržovat, vrať se mezi ně, já též hned odjedu.' – Pan Prošek se poklonil, netroufaje si velitelku svoji zdržovat ... [*Babička*, Praha, 1968, 126]

2a/ 'Kde je váš čeledín?' 'Doma, prosím, v Rybárech.' 'Jak to víte?' 'Nu, – myslím si jen –' 'Neptám se, co si myslíte. Jak víte, že je v Rybárech?' '– Nevím.' [ČH, 86–7]
2b/ Pán je cizí? Ano, to jest, cizí, právě se nastěhoval a nezná to tu ještě, bude tu trvale bydlet. Pak ovšem ... bude potřebovat tu a tam vyprat prádlo. Sehnal si už v Dolině nějakou ženu, která by mu prala? Vida, ... na to dosud ani nevzpomměl, a je to důležitá věc. [VF, 56]

3/ Děkuje oběma pánům srdečně za dobrou vůli; ale ví, že jeho spor je v nejlepších rukou a prosí doktora Sacka, aby za něho jednal. [PF, 99]

4/ Snad má pán několik párů bot, které si nestačil očistit v těchto mizerných dnech, vycídili by mu je tak, že by se leskly jak zrcadlo. Nechtějí za to peníze, ale byli by vděčni za trochu chleba ... [VF, 382]

5/ 'Jak se máte, Eržiko?' ... Ne, nemusí se bát, nejde služebně. [ON, 147]

6/ Přivedou-li mu Nikolu, dostanou na pálenku. Ne-li, půjdou ihned k odvodu a na frontu. [ON, 33]

7/ Co si pomyslí parta, – každý udělal stokrát víc, i to zvíře Matula, i Pepek se svou držkou. [ČF, 208–9]

8/ Znal ji. Je citlivá, proměnlivá jako jarní počasí, výbušná a v zápětí zasněně zjihlá. A tvrdohlavá! Přímým bojem neprorazíš, ale znáš-li ji, hraješ na klávesnici jejích nálad a slabůstek jako mistr. [OC, 93]

9/ Děkuji, zatím nehladovím, jak vidí, pan Pohořelý se o mne znamenitě stará. [VF, 152]

10/ Mohli bychom se potom přestěhovat dolů ke mně, kde nebudeme nikoho rušit. [VF, 130]

11/ Domníval se, že kupuje zboží kompletní. [VF, 297]

12/ Hrávají vždycky v sobotu nebo před svátkem, když se nemusí nazítří vstávat ... [VF, 129]

13/ Nemám-li volné chvilky na vymýšlení ... měl bych obálku aspoň ovázat nějakou stužkou nebo nařídit Blance, aby to udělala. [VF, 67]

14/ Dovolím-li tedy, abychom nezapomněli na účel mé návštěvy, přesvědčí se především o čísle mého límečku a o rozměrech mého pasu a rukávu. [VF, 297]

15/ Teď jenom je hlavní věc, abychom nebyli příliš přísní, až se vrátí ... Rozhodně máme ihned zatelefonovat, jak přijde domů, aby se nestarali zbytečně. [VF, 72]

16/ Dvě a půl hodiny bychom měli pro sebe, prostudovala to v jízdním řádě. [VF, 329]

17/ Nemohla by paní Slávka klepnout za krk nějakého pěkného králíčka? ... Nemá paní Slávka nějaký košík na hřiby, který by mohla nějaký den postrádat? [VF, 330]

18/ Takové vojsko se valí cesta necesta, vjedou s tanky na pole, koně poženou rovnou přes obilí. [VF, 152]

19/ Gamza má přirozeně kritickou svobodu ve své divadelní rubrice. Vlach je dalek toho, aby mu do ní zasahoval. [PF, 166]

20/ Byli zrazeni a měli být zavražděni. Nikola měl býti zavražděn. [ON, 162]

21/ Prádlo přiveze co nejdříve. [VF, 57]

22/ 'Otec je v poli?' Ne, byl doma ... [ON, 28]

23/ Ach, tma byla stejně lepší k tomu, nač se chtěl ptát. [PP, 79]

Tak tohle byla Růža ... To byla její Růženka, na které si kdysi zakládala. [PL, 176]

24/ Má čekat až ve Volovém nebo v Chustě, kde jeho postavení bude o hodně horší než zde? [ON, 76]

25/ Mohli by odtud zavolat, aby tam na to místo přijel nákladák nebo aspoň motocykl? [VF, 380]

26/ Ale proboha, tudy přece nemůže domů, stezka je pod vodou. [VF, 403]

27/ Ten potok je zřejmě jeho potok a zavede ho po proudu zrovna domů. [VF, 62]

28/ Tento průkaz ... už paní zajisté několikrát viděla. [PF, 64]

29/ Či působila [větvička] jen za války a nyní už její síla pominula? [ON, 62]

30/ Byly dnes u slečny Kazmarové propuštěné přadleny? [PP, 287]

31/ Letos v dubnu dostali pumu a nenašli z nikoho ani kousek. [VF, 383]

32/ Konečně! Zítra nebo pozítří půjde k Petru Šuhajovi. [ON, 73]

33/ Ať jí Jarmila také poděkuje, paní byla tak laskavá ... [PPr, 107]

34/ Jen ať se Nella přesvědčí, babička dobře přiklopila kahánek. [PF, 23]

35/ Mohl by mu Jasinko přivézti asi čtyři fůry dříví? [ON, 214]

36/ Jenže kam odhodila [prababička] hořící sirku? [PF, 23]

37/ Ví slečna Kazmarová, že protestní schůze proti výpovědem u Kazmara byla původně svolána do Úlů? [PP, 287]

38/ Přijela Torglerova matka; dovolí předseda soudu, aby byla přítomna při líčení? [PF, 93]

39/ Fuj! Přece by se s ním raději zase shledal tu na pitevním stole než v Chustě. [ON, 223]

40/ Opona, odolávající ohni! Že na tu nevzpomněli dřív! ... Té se Ondřej nastahoval! [PP, 270]

41/ Mají na koktajly, a nemají na mlékaře! Mají na benzin, a nemají na podrážky! Vždyť je to obrácený svět! [PP, 64]

42/ Ach, kéž by také oni mohli bohatým bráti a chudým dávati! Kéž by také oni mohli mstíti lidskou křivdu! [ON, 250–1]

43/ Děje se něco? Ulétá Eržika? Ano, něco se děje. [ON, 147]

44/ Co udělá, až jí poví, že ji opustí? Pohne řasami, zbledne, budou se jí třást ruce, jako za vánoční jízdy do Nechleb? [PP, 179]

45/ Je tak úžasně sladká! [ON, 149]

46/ A vždyť by se na smrt styděla cizího muže, který je ke všemu takový dobrý známý a hodný člověk. [PP, 60–1]

47/ Dimitrov zneužívá lavice obžalovaných za tribunu zhoubných marxistických hesel. [PF, 92]

48/ Jak bylo možno s kouzelnou větvičkou žít tak bídně a uboze? [ON, 62]

49/ Proklatí cizinci! Němec by tohle neudělal. [PF, 117]

50/ Nemusí se teď vůbec pustit do tak prašivé věci. [VF, 353]

51/ Otec také uteče. Odvede dobytek na poloninu, matku s malými dětmi nechá někde tam a odejde do Polska nebo do Rumunska. [ON, 131]

52/ Za takových okolností si ovšem knížku rád přečte, on i jeho žena, chlapci taky. [VF, 20]

53/ Něco povídala Liduška, že prý je [Miškeřík] v drachovském blázinci. [PP, 262]

54/ Dal se fascinovat jménem Nikola Šuhaj, stejně jako všichni ti hlupáci zde. [ON, 223]

55 / Aby se Nella neujímala té maškary! [PF, 21]

56/ Co asi teď dělá, chudák, ten blázen ... [PP, 202]

57/ Ten potok je zřejmě jeho potok a zavede ho po proudu zrovna domů. Za čtvrt hodiny vyšel z lesa a stál před Dolinou, ale docela v jiném koutě; byl to jiný potok. [VF, 62]

58/ Má v sobě boží moc. A ta ho nezradí. [ON, 135]

59/ K obhajobě se už Gamza nedostane, to je jasné. [PF, 107]

60/ Ach, zbabělci. Patrně je nechtěli najít! Patrně jim bylo velmi příjemno, že banditi stále střídají místa. [ON, 167]

61/ Třeba se od žabáka něco doví o Karlovi. [PP, 338]

62/ Řekla-li to majdanská čarodějnice, je to pravda. [ON, 150]

63/ Nemůže mlčet, musí aspoň něco podotknout. [VF, 82]

64/ Prostě – netouží po tom, chce mít klid k práci a nic víc. [OC, 31]

65/ Autostrády, ty jim Hospodář záviděl. [PP, 244]

66/ Je zdejším učitelem, jednotřídka – měl před svatbou, dokonce už i nábytek – jmenovala se Anežka. [VF, 81]

67/ Ale paní Ró si přeje něco stylového, vždyť to říká. [PF, 8]

68/ Předsedu senátu by spíše zajímalo vědět, kolik bylo třeba řečené tekutiny na zapálení velké síně. [PF, 118]

69/ 'Byly – jakési řeči,' mumlá Juraj. 'O tobě ... a o čeledínovi ... Tak to nemůže zůstat, Polano.' 'Proč?' vyhrkla prudce Polana. 'K vůli těm hloupým řečem?' [ČH, 59]

70/ Proč toho výrostka ještě neodvedli, myslil si Nikola, a jímal ho hněv, jest jen o rok mladší než já a sedmnáct mu již bylo?! [ON, 29]

71/ Že toto bývalo pole Hordubalovo? Pravda, že bývalo – samý kámen prý a přece tu sklidil Pjosa žito, brambory tu má a políčko lnu; vida, jak se spojilo Pjosovo pole s Hordubalovým! [ČH, 40]

72/ Jen se mu [Nikolovi] ještě kmitla hlavou slova: 'Nic se mi nestane. Mám takovou moc od Boha.' [ON, 122]

73/ [Prokop] se pustil na policejní ředitelství, oddělení dotazy. Jiří Tomeš, listoval zaprášený oficiál v knihách, inženýr Tomeš Jiří, to je, prosím, na Smíchově, ulice ta a ta. Byla to patrně stará adresa. Nicméně letěl Prokop na Smíchov do ulice té a té. Domovník kroutil hlavou, když se ho ptal po Jiřím Tomši. Toť že tu ten jistý bydlel, ale už víc než před rokem; kde bydlí teď, neví nikdo. [ČK, 101]

74/ Tady je Brych! Sháním vás už hodinu ... na vaši paní už to přišlo ... ano, sehnal jsem lékaře, všechno je v pořádku ... ne, jen klid, všechno klape ... [OC, 40]

75/ Vedoucí pánové strany se sjeli do Berlína k politické poradě, jak jí bylo občas třeba, aby nacionální socialisté zachovali jednotnou linii ve volební kampani ... Vůdce u něho právě večeřel, a rozhovor u stolu byl jako obvykle živý a srdečný, když vyzvali hostitele k telefonu. Volal ho doktor Hanfstängel, vedoucí zahraniční tiskové služby, že hoří sněmovna. [PF, 127]

76/ 'Pane vrátný, když jste otvíral Torglerovi sněmovní vrata číslo pět, necítil jste z něho nějaký zvláštní zápach? ...' Ne, vrátný nic nepozoroval na panu poslanci Torglerovi, když vycházel něco po osmé ze sněmovny. [PF, 116, 117]

77/ 'Běž se domů převléknout do lidských šatů,' poručil 'a pospěš si!' Počká tu na ni. Chvíli se spolu projdou. [PPR, 28]

78/ Proč se jí pořád do všeho pletou? Vždyť nemají ponětí, co je doopravdy život. Co s nimi mám společného? Já jsem jenom já. A je to možná, že s těmihle kluky někdy hrála 'Člověče, nezlob se'? [PPr, 38]

79/ Třeba se od žabáka něco doví o Karlovi, třeba se žabák o ní podřekne samým nadšením Karlovi, Karel žárlí, Karel se trápí, Karel šíleně trpí, Karel ji znovu miluje, Karle, Karle, jak jsi mně to mohl udělat, ty nevíš, co je láska ... [PP, 338]

80/ Oba přátele našel [Beer] u Jasinků samotné. Smrákalo se již a déšť činil jizbu temnou. Mohl by mu Jasinko přivézti asi čtyři fůry dříví? Proč ne? Zítra? Dobře. Pak se Abram Beer posadil v koutě na lavici: 'Prší.' 'Prší.' [ON, 214]

81/ Vašek ho upřeně pozoruje, neřekne ani slovo. Tatík ho vůbec nepřekvapil, taky na to pomyslel. Co na to říci? Nic! To se uvidí, rozmyslím si to cestou. [OC, 56]

82/ Na nejbližším rohu zůstal [Prokop] stát: Co teď? Zbývá jen Carson. Neznámá veličina, jež o něčem ví a něco chce. Dobrá, tedy Carson. Prokop nahmatal v kapse lístek, jejž zapomněl poslat, a rozběhl se na poštu. Ale u poštovní schránky mu klesla ruka. Carson, Carson, – ano, ale tomu jde o cosi, co ... také není maličkost ... Proč vůbec mne shání? Patrně Tomeš neví vše ... Tak to asi je; ale (a tu se Prokop poprvé zhrozil dosahu věci) což je vůbec možno vyrukovat s Krakatitem ven? ... Prokopovi začalo být z celé věci až úzko. Který čert sem nese toho zatraceného Carsona? Pro Krista Pana, musí se stůj co stůj zabránit – [ČK, 107–8]

83/ Rytmus chůze probouzel vzpomínky a ty se k sobě řadily jako jeho kroky. Měl opravdu zelenou větvičku? ... Měl takový dar? Ano, měl takový dar! Až Nikolu při té odpovědi zamrazilo v zádech. Křik dětí dávno dozněl. Snad se opravdu mohl státi Oleksou Dovbušem. Snad opravdu opustil svou slávu pro ženu ... Chůze Nikoly Šuhaje se stávala pomalou. Země byla rozměklá a jeho kroků nebylo slyšeti ... Jak bylo možno s kouzelnou větvičkou v ruce žíti tak bídně a uboze? [ON, 61–2]

84/ Ředitel Vykoukal přehlíží armádu generálským okem, modrým hněvem, něco ho dnes hněte, něco soukromého, syn je pro zlost, co je komu po tom. [PP, 311]

85/ Ano, Juraj přišel k Nikolovi a zůstane u něho. [ON, 131]

86/ Ale on, Brych, nemůže. [OC, 216]

87/ Nikola opět hledí do kraje. Tam dole leží Koločava: roztáhlá řada drobtů, jež by bylo možno smésti rukama na hromádku a vzíti do misky dlaně. [ON, 162]

88/ Koločava je prokletá obec. Tak trochu podobná sibiřským vesnicím. Žije se tu jako v obsazeném území, pohledy lidí jsou posupné a výsměšné zároveň ... [ON, 148]

89/ Také matka synů odsouzených na smrt lámala chléb a jedla; vyhladoví jako každý člověk, a snad ji přemůže únava a v noci spí; nelze člověku bdít rok; dokonce možná, ti uvěznění hoši, ... že i ti někdy usínají, a jakými asi sny! [PP, 103]

90/ Když Helenka dodělávala praktikum na ortopedii, ležel na sále mladý člověk, který si zlomil stehenní kost. Taková běžná fraktura femoru, žádný zajímavý případ. [PF, 24]

91/ Možná, že to bylo ještě živé, ta zvířata, co jedli Häusler s Růžou syrová. Ondřej by to nevzal do úst za svět. Ale Růža, která již na Štědrý večer v Nechlebách tak statečně rozkousala hlemýždě za povzbuzování jiného starého pána, strýce Františka, polykala teď ústřice, ten hnusný sliz, na který se Ondřej nemohl ani podívat, pomocí kapky citrónu, a chtěla zapít vínem. [PP, 413]

92/ Vyšel snad v Brazách ze země Dovbušův kris? Tam před smrtí slavný loupežník těchto hor zakopal svou křesací ručnici hluboko. A puška se každého roku posouvá o znání z temnot k zemskému povrchu a až na slunci zasvítí celá, jako z jara na polonině kuklík nebo sasanka, vzejde světu nový Oleksa Dovbuš, který bohatým bral, chudým dával, pral pány a nikdy nikoho nezabil, leč ze spravedlivé msty nebo v sebeobraně. [ON, 82–3]

2 / Composition of *The Labyrinth of the World and the Paradise of the Heart* by Jan A. Komenský (Comenius)

1/ Někteří zajisté sbírali smetí a rozdělovali mezi sebe; někteří se s kládím a kamením sem a tam váleli aneb je po skřipcích vzhůru leckams tahali a zpouštěli zase; někteří kopali zemi a převáželi neb přenášeli z místa na místo; ostatek lidu se zvonci, zrcadly, měchýři, hrkavkami a jinými titěrkami zacházeli; někteří i s svým stínem hráli, jej měříce, honíce, lapajíce. A to vše tak úsilně, až mnozí sténali a potili se, někteří se i přetrhovali. [25]

2/ Vejdeme tedy do ulice: a aj, množství těch lidí, vše po páru, než mnoho, jakž mi se zdálo, velmi nerovné spřeže, hrubých s malými, pěkných s mrzkými, mladých s starými etc. A hledě já pilně, co pak dělají a v čem by taková ta toho stavu sladkost záležela, vidím, ani na sebe hledí, s sebou mluví, někdy jeden druhého pohladí, někdy i políbí. [32]

3/ Uhlédal sem také jiný neřád, slepotu a bláznovství. [26]

4/ Pomyslil sem sobě toliko: 'Divná toho světa zpráva! Král žena, raddy ženy, úředníci ženy, všecken regiment ženský! Což se ho kdo báti má!' [112]

5/ Jakýchž řečí já doslýchaje, počal sem i sám vesel býti, a že se i mně bohdá toho, nač se jiní brousí, dostane, naději sobě činiti ... Odtud pak jeden sobě zoufal, druhý se ohlédaje a k vyslídění jejich nových cest ohleduje, znovu se trápil, až mne samého konce se dočkati nemohoucího teskno bylo ... 'A což z toho všeho nic býti má? Ach, mé naděje!' [64, 65, 66]

6/ Řekl sem: 'To je pěkná věc!' ale podívaje se trošku, zošklivil sem ji sobě. [68]

7/ Což vida řekl sem: 'Toť jest bláznovství, že tito z vůdců a rádců svých následovníky a pochlebníky míti chtějí.' 'Tak jest světa běh,' řekl tlumočník; 'a neškodí to. Kdyby volavcům těm všecko volno bylo, kdo ví, čeho by sobě oni neosvobodili?' [75]

8/ 'I což to bude?' dím já. On: 'Academia bude korunovati ty, kteříž nad jiné byvše pilnější, vrchu umění dosáhli.' [69]

9/ I ptal sem se: 'Kdo sou to a co dělají?' Odpověděl mi: 'Nejsubtýlnější filozofi, kteříž, co slunce nebeské horkostí svou v střevách země za několik let zpraviti nemůž, dopravují, kovy všelijaké na nejvyšší stupeň vyvodíce, to jest na zlato.' 'A načiž je to?' řekl sem; 'Však se víc železa a jiných kovů než zlata užívá.' 'Cos ty bloud!' řekl on. 'Vždyť jest zlato nejvzácnější věc, kdo je má, chudoby se nebojí.' [61]

10/ 'Ty muderlantství nepřestaneš, ... leč sobě něco utržíš.' [70]

'Nepřestaneš-li mudrování, octneš se kde by nerád.' [83]

'Ej, nemudruj tak příliš, ... věř jiným víc než sobě.' [97]

11/ 'Ale tohoť o tobě neráda slyším, že tak cosi vybíravého jsi, a učiti se jakožto novotný v světě host maje, ty se v mudrování vydáváš.' [111]

12/ ... poněvadž nejmoudřejší ze všech, Šalomoun, rozum svůj poddal a řádům světa, jak to tu každý vidí, obvyká, proč oni vytrhovati se a přes to mudrovati mají? [126]

13/ 'Nyní ty zvíš, ... jak bývá těm, kteříž mudrováním svým roty a bouře v světě začínají.' [126]

14/ 'Již vidím, že v světě lépe nebude! Jižť je po mé naději veta! Běda mně!' [127]

15/ 'Viděls v druhém stavu, jakými se neskonalými pracemi lidé, zisku hledajíce, zanášejí, jakých fortelů chytají, jakých nebezpečenství odvažují. Ty kvaltování ta všecka za marnost měj, věda, že jednoho toliko potřebí jest, přízně Boží. A protož ty jediného povolání, kteréžť sem svěřil, ostříhaje, věrně, upřímě, tiše práci svou veď, konec a cíl všeho mně poroučeje.' [132]

'Onino v hojném kvasu, jídle, pití, smíchu radost zakládají: tobě milo buď se mnou a pro mne, když toho potřebí, lačněti, žízniti, plakati, rány a všecko trpěti.' [135]

16/ Těmto zajisté zodjímaje Bůh srdce kamenná, massitá dal do těla, ohebná a povolná ke všeliké vůli Boží. A ač jim těch i jiných nesnadností ďábel lstivými vnukáními, svět pohoršitedlnými příklady, tělo přirozenou svou k dobrému váhavostí nemálo dělají, oni však toho nic nedbají, ďábla střelbou modliteb odhánějíce, světu štítem nepromenného úmyslu se zamítajíce, tělo bičem kázně ku poslušenství doháněíce ... Já sem neviděl, aby kdo mezi těmito mdlobou těla osvobozování sobě hříchu zastával; anebo křehkostí přirození spáchanou zlost vymlouval. Než viděl sem, že když kdo cele srdce tomu, kterýž je stvořil, vykoupil a za chrám posvětil, oddal, za srdcem již jiní oudové povolně a povlovně, kam Bůh chtěl, tak se klonili. Ó křesťané, kdož jsi koli, dobuď se z okovů těla, ohledej, zkus a poznej, že překážky, kteréž sobě v mysli maluješ, menší jsou, nežli aby vůli tvé, jestliže opravdová jest, zbrániti mohly. [148–9]

17/ Pravili také, že svět svým vlastním rovně neodpouští, své vlastní škrabe, šidí, loupí, trápí, i nechť prý nám to též dělá, herež. Nemůžeme-li trýzněni toho prázdni býti, tu je snášeti chceme, kdež by se nám od světa nahodilé škody Božskou štědrou dobrotou vynahraditi mohly: a tak se nám smích jejich, nenávist, křivdy a škody v zisk obrátí. [145]

Proč by se tím křesťan trápil, kterýž svědomí své spořádané a v srdci Boží milost má? Nechtějí-li se k našim obyčejům formovati lidé, formujme se my k jejich, pokud jen pro svědomí lze. Svět ze zlého v horší jde, pravda jest: ale zdaž my to fresováním svým napravíme? [155]

18/ Všecko tu světu naodpor sem spatřil. V světě zajisté všudy slepotu a mrákotu, tuto jasné světlo sem spatřil; v světě šalbu, tuto pravdu; v světě neřádů plno, tuto sám ušlechtilý řád; v světě kvaltování, tuto pokoj, v světě starosti a fresuňky, tuto radost; v světě nedostatky, tuto hojnost; v světě otroctví a porobu, tuto svobodu ... [139]

Jakž sem prve v světě mnoho kolotání a lopotování, fresuňků a starostí, hrůz a strachu všudy po všech stavích znamenal, tak sem tuto mnoho pokojné a dobré mysli při všechněch Bohu oddaných nalezl. [153]

Místo oněch ocelivých pout viděl sem tuto zlaté zápony; místo trhání se od sebe potěšené těl i srdcí spojení. [158]

In footnotes:
7 Jeho prvá část líčí obrazně hříčky a marnosti tohoto světa, kterak se on ve všem všudy obírá s velkým úsilím věcmi malichernými a jak žalostně všecko nakonec mění v posměch nebo v pláč. Druhá část popisuje zčásti jinotajně, zčásti zjevně pravé a trvalé štěstí Božích synů: jak vskutku jsou blaženi ti, kdo odvrátivše se od světa a všech světských věcí, jedině k samému Bohu přilnou, ba do něho velnou. [9]

13 Některé (smrt) poranila toliko, pochromila, oslepila, ohlušila nebo omráčila. [28]

21 Viděl sem, viděl, viděl a poznal, že Boha s nebeskými jeho poklady v sobě míti slavnějšího cosi jest ... [157]

3 / The objective narrator:
Kaliba's Crime by Karel V. Rais

1/ Po modré, čím blíže k slunci tím bělejší obloze se přeháněla světlá oblaka; jak některý mráček přes slunce přelétal, jak se jiné k němu blížily, osvětlení krajiny se měnilo, stíny se přehupovaly a měnily i barvy starého hvozdu. Hned bylo všechno tmavší, hned jednotlivá místa jasněji zasvítila. Zelená, hnědá, žlutá barva se ukazovaly ve všech svých odstínech. [25]

Rozletěly se chumle sněhových mrakův a modré nebe se rozklenulo nad zemí. Slunce se na blankytě roztřáslo, ale po kopcovité krajině bylo jediné bělo sněhové, jímž se země, opět na kost utuhlá, ještě obalila. [77]

Obzor byl velmi vysoký a čistý. – Nad měkkými hrudami polí tejnořili skřivani, vznášela se hejna bílých, rusých i tmavých holubů, jejichž křídla se svitem slunečním jen leskla. Po mezích si vykračovaly popelavé vrány a černí krkavčíci bílých odřených zobanů se hrabali v prsti. – Vlahý východní vítr promočenou ornici, cesty i louky rychle vysoušel a rozčechrával prořídlý les. [144]

2/ O veřeje stál opřen mladý Kaliba, veliký, silný, ramenatý, snad asi pětatřicátník. Na mohutné kulaté hlavě měl rozházeny kaštanové chundely měkkých vlasů, nízké čelo s třemi hlubokými rýhami, velké modré, poněkud vypoulené oči. Tváře měl plné, zdravě červené, opálené. Byl v krátké vlněné kazajce, a nohavice měl zastrčeny do vysokých odřených holínek. [10]

Byla ještě statná zdravá panímáma, ačkoliv tváře i čelo měla vráskami notně rozryty. Byla v tmavé jupce, v krátké pruhované vlňačce, pod níž bylo viděti bílé punčochy a sametové střevíce. Šátek na hlavě měla uvázaný na kretku, černé vlasy rozděleny k spánkům. Smějíc se, ukazovala, že má v dásních již jenom několik silných zubů. [30–1]

3/ Byla hezká, jenom oči jí chvílemi divně zasvítily, řasy se zchmuřily a pohled pak nabyl zvláštního divokého, skoro škaredivého výrazu, jenž upomínal na matku. [34]

4/ Vojta byl ale rozmrzen; s tím včerejškem se naň všeho sesypalo trochu mnoho, nebyl tomu zvyklý a nevěděl, kudy z toho ven. Tatínek, Nána, panímáma – se všech stran se to hrne. Jaktěživ v ničem takovém nebyl! [126]

5/ Zlá myšlenka mu projela hlavou. – 'Snad je tam ten voják Rachota – proč by se nevracely?' Již si naň dávno ani dost málo nevzpomněl – ale proč, proč by se nevracely? – Při té myšlence zatal pěsti, prudce dýchal a na jednom místě vydržeti nemohl. [135]

6/ Ale [Vojta] neusínal ... – Klenba nebeská, potemnělá, jen řídce prostřiknutá jemně zářícím hvězdným květem, rozpínala se nad ním jako plášť hrozného zvonu, na jehož srdci oddychoval ... – Vojta stále hleděl k obloze. Časem mu lícem přeletěl jemný van, jako by jej polil, to byl tichý pozdrav starého lesa, který ze sna několikrát prudčeji zadýchal. [186]

7/ Vojta stál za svojí chalupou ... – Tu je stodola – tam se probělává stěna tatínkova vejměnku ... – Ten vejměnek je tak smutný, tmavý – a na druhé straně ve stavení bude beztoho taky tak ... –Rychleji přešel dvorek – opřel se o starou jabloň, jež se skláněla ke střeše nad světnicí, a jako na přivítanou sypala naň chumelici bílého kvítí sněhového. – Vystoupiv na špičky, tělo naklonil vpřed a zíral do světnice ... –Aj – na lavici pod oknem do návsi sedí panímáma a směje se – řehtavě se směje, a oči jí svítí. – Krok stačil a Vojta stál u samé stěny ... – Na okamžik zahlédl Karlu – něco hovořila, ale ne k panímámě – Ještě někdo tam byl. [235–6]

4 / Karel Čapek and Vladislav Vančura:
An essay in comparative stylistics

1/ Pak tam přišli dva lidé, mužský se ženskou, ale neviděli mne; seděli zády ke mně a tiše hovořili ... Nejdřív hovořili hodně staccato; potom začal ten mužský pomalu a tiše něco vykládat, jako by to z něho nechtělo ven; a pak to rychle vysypal. Ta ženská vykřikla hrůzou a něco mu rozčileně říkala; ale on jí sevřel ruku, až zaúpěla, a začal jí mezi zuby domlouvat. Poslouchejte, to nebyl milostný hovor, to muzikant pozná; milostné přemlouvání má docela jinou kadenci a nezní tak jaksi sevřeně, – milostný hovor je hluboké cello, ale tohle byla vysoká basa, hraná takovým presto rubato, v jediné poloze, jako kdyby ten člověk pořád opakoval jednu věc ... Ta ženská začala tiše plakat ... měla trochu klarinetový, dřevěný hlas, který nezněl tuze mladě ... Tu ten mužský hlas se jal bručet velmi hluboko, čistě basově a skoro zamilovaně; ženský pláč přešel do drobného a pasivního vzlyku; to znamená, že byl odpor zlomen ... [*Povídky z druhé kapsy*, Praha, 1967, 68–9]

2/ Tu přišla Josefina a vloživši chladnou dlaň na jeho hněv, odpověděla mu:

'Všechno, co řekneš, Jene, je málo. Až se otevrou dveře tohoto mlýna, kam půjdeme? Zlost je jediná chvíle, avšak jídlo a byt jsou čas. Jericho nepadne křikem.'

'Věc je rozhodnuta,' řekl Jan, 'nezůstaneme v Nadelhotách. Je opět čas, Josefino, abychom vzali svoje věci a stěhovali se.'

'Nelituji toho,' odpověděla, 'ale jinde nebude lépe. Jsme chudí a jest nám sloužiti na všech místech ...' [*Pekař Jan Marhoul*, Praha, 1947, 115–6]

3/ 'Bohatství! Bohatství nad touhu srdce! Každý den bývám trestán a každého jitra se modlím. Otče nášjenž jsi na nebesích, dej mi peníze a poklady, jež skrýváš. Budu na roveň proti štěstí pyšných a proti štěstí ukrutníka, který mne bije, ačkoliv odvádím peníze, jichž si žádá. Budu vypravovat věci takové, neboť jsem je viděl, vešed do příbytku nejbohatšího ...' [*Pole orná a válečná*, Praha, 1947, 71]

4/ Nepopřál jsem jí v tomto ohledu sluchu, ale teď, když jsem stár, chápu, že se v jejích radách tajilo jádro rozumné. [*Konec starých časů*, Praha, 1947, 152]

Přišed domů, odložil jsem šat a hotovil jsem se ulehnout. [*Ibid.*, 221]

Řkouc to odběhla nežádajíc si odpovědi. [*Ibid.*, 353]

5/ Ostatně nevěřím na nemastná a neslaná vypravování. Na rozdíl od licoměrníků a lidí bez chuti tvrdím, že každý příběh má být kořeněn láskou a nenávistí. Má čpěti po kotlíku, v němž byl uvařen, má býti tak vypravován, abyste poznali jeho kuchaře, jako piják vína pozná vinici, kde se urodila jeho láhev. [*Ibid.*, 10]

6/Bylo jí asi kolem třiceti, ach to jsou krásná léta! Tehdy se boky paniček zakulacují, jejich prsy se stávají těžkými a snižují se. Neříkám, že by patnáct let nebylo lepší než tato třicítka, ale v tak raném mládí se nepospíchá, a to se nám nehodí do krámu. [*Luk královny Dorotky*, Praha, 1947, 96–7]

7/ Vám je radostí sledovati milenku v rozletu hudby? Jste si jist, že hraje překrásně Beethovena? Ale vaši sousedé vypravují, že tříská do klavíru, až jim zaléhají uši. Ach, to je příliš těžká věc, shodnouti se o tom, co je krásné a slušné. Konec konců lze Isabellu a Cypriana obhajovati. Ba věru, my je obhájíme na váš účet, vy šibalové a krasoduché dámy, již všichni hřešíte v myšlenkách jako kozy a kozlové. Jediné, co vám dodává zdání zdrženlivosti, je chatrné tělo, neboť můžete uskutečniti pouhou polovinu svých snů. [*Ibid.*, 115]

8/ Po desáté hodině vyšla sama princezna, provázena následníkem trůnu a zamířila někam k japonskému pavilónu. V Prokopovi hrklo, zdálo se mu, že letí hlavou dolů; křečovitě se chytil větve a třásl se jako list. Nikdo nešel za nimi; naopak všichni kolem vyklidili park a zdržovali se na prostranství před zámkem. Asi rozhodující rozmluva nebo co. Prokop se kousal do rtů, aby nevykřikl. Trvalo to nesmírně dlouho, snad hodinu, nebo pět hodin. A teď běží odtamtud následník sám, je rudý a zatíná pěstě. [*Krakatit*, Praha, 1924, 187]

9/ Londýnská ulice je jen takové koryto, kterým život teče, aby už byl doma. [*Anglické listy*, Praha, 1960, 79]

Jen Ovce, Krávy a Koně žvýkají krásu přírody rozmyslně a beze spěchu. [*Ibid.*, 141]

10/ Highlandři stojí v pozoru, za nimi hrad skotských králů a ještě dále za nimi celé krvavé a strašné dějiny této země. [*Ibid.*, 121]

Jen anglický trávník a anglický gentleman se denně holí. [*Ibid.*, 156]

11/ Hora pil a obrazu i kořalky ubývalo, až prázdná sklenice přikryla nos pijákův, jako poklop zahradníkův kryje klíček chřestu. [*Pole orná a válečná*, 12]

Věž chrámu zdvihající se z města hloupě a drze, jako by výšiny nebe, do nichž ukazovala svou jehlovitou špicí, nebyly bezduché a jako by v těchto končinách něco trvalo. V provazišti noci se tetelily hvězdy příliš hrozné, aby byly útěchou a po dně města lezli obžerové do svých hospod. [*Ibid.*, 210]

Smrt. To je to slovo, to je ten zvuk, to je to šelestění, to je ten motýl, který se vznáší mezi světly a bije křídly. [*Tři řeky*, Praha, 1958, 173]

5 / 'Narrative symposium' in Milan Kundera's *The Joke*

1/ Vystupovali jsme na stovkách koncertů a estrád, zpívali jsme sovětské písně, naše budovatelské písně a ovšem lidové písně, ty jsme zpívali nejraději, moravské písně jsem si tehdy tak zamilovala, že jsem se cítila já, Plzeňačka, Moravankou, staly se leitmotivem mého života ... [20]

A potom jsme seděli v malé hospůdce u Zbraslavi, jedli jsme chleba a buřt, všechno bylo docela obyčejné a prosté, nevrlý hostinský, politý ubrus, a přece to bylo nádherné dobrodružství ...[27]

2/ Tvrdil jste kdysi, že socialismus vyrostl na kmeni evropského racionalismu a skepticismu, na kmeni nenáboženském a protináboženském a není jinak myslitelný. Ale chcete opravdu dál vážně tvrdit, že bez víry v prvotnost hmoty nelze vybudovat socialistickou společnost? Myslíte opravdu, že lidé věřící v Boha nemohou znárodnit továrny? [215]

3/ Čeština se stáhla z měst na venkov a patřila jen negramotným. I mezi nimi však nepřestala tvořit dál svou kulturu. Kulturu skromničkou a zrakům Evropy docela skrytou. Kulturu písní, pohádek, zvykových obřadů, přísloví a řikadel. [124–5]

4/ Vyšli jsme tedy z nemocnice a brzo došli ke skupině novostaveb, které nesouladně trčely jedna vedle druhé z neurovnaného prašného terénu (bez trávníku, bez chodníku, bez silnice) a tvořily smutnou scenérii na konci města hraničícího s prázdnou rovinou dalekých polí. Vešli jsme do jedněch dveří, stoupali po úzkém schodišti (výtah nefungoval) a zastavili se až ve třetím poschodí. [10]

5/ Od onoho večera se ve mně všechno změnilo; byl jsem opět obydlen; nebyl jsem už jen tou žalostnou prázdnotou, v níž se proháněly (jak smetí ve vyrabovaném pokoji) stesky, výčitky a žaloby; pokoj mého nitra byl náhle uklizen a kdosi v něm žil. Hodiny, které v něm na stěně visely s rafičkami po dlouhé měsíce nepohnutými, se pojednou roztikaly. [70]

Bibliography

1 LINGUISTICS AND STYLISTICS

BENVENISTE, E. 'De la subjectivité dans le langage', *Journal de psychologie*, (Jul.–Sept. 1958). [Reprinted in: *Problèmes de linguistique général*. Paris, 1966.]

BÜHLER, K. *Sprachtheorie*. Jena, 1934.

CHATMAN, S., S. R. LEVIN (eds.). *Essays on the Language of Literature*. Boston, 1967.

DOKULIL, M. 'K modální výstavbě věty', *Studie a práce linguistické*, vol. I. Prague, 1954.

DOLEŽEL, L. 'Vers la stylistique structurale', *Travaux linguistique de Prague*, vol. I. Prague, 1964.

GREIMAS, A.J. 'Les topologiques', *Cahiers de lexicologie*, IV (1964).

– *Sémantique structurale*. Paris, 1966.

ISAČENKO, A.V. 'O prizyvnoj funkcii jazyka', *Recueil linguistique de Bratislava*. Bratislava, 1948.

JAKOBSON, R. 'Efforts toward a Means-End Model in Interwar Continental Linguistics', *Trends in Modern Linguistics*, vol. II. Utrecht, 1963.

– 'Grammatical Parallelism and its Russian Facet', *Language*, XLII (April–June, 1966).

– 'Linguistics and Poetics', *Style in Language*. T.A. Sebeok (ed.). New York, 1960.

– *Shifters, Verbal Categories and the Russian Verb*. Cambridge, Mass., 1957.

JEDLIČKA, A. 'K charakteristice syntaxe současné spisovné češtiny', *Slavica Pragensia*, x (Acta Universitatis Carolinae, Philologica 1–3, 1968).

SPITZER, L. *Stilstudien*, I–II. Munich, 1928.

TRÁVNÍČEK, F. *Mluvnice spisovné češtiny*. 3rd ed. Prague, 1951.

VINOGRADOV, V.V. *Stiľ Puškina*. Moscow, 1941.

VOLOŠINOV, V.N. *Marksizm i filosofija jazyka*. Leningrad, 1930.

2 THEORY OF LITERATURE

CURTIUS, E.R. *Europäische Literatur und lateinisches Mittelalter*. Bern, 1948.

ERLICH, V. *Russian Formalism. History – Doctrine*. 2nd ed. The Hague, 1965.

– 'The Concept of the Poet as a Problem of Poetics', *Poetics-Poetyka-Poetika*. Warsaw – The Hague, 1961.

FRYE, N. *Anatomy of Criticism*. 8th ed. New York, 1969.

JANKOVIČ, M., Z. PEŠAT, F. VODIČKA (eds.). *Struktura a smysl literárního díla*. Prague, 1966.

LEMON, L., M. J. REIS (eds.). *Russian Formalist Criticism*. Lincoln, Nebraska, 1965.

MATEJKA, L. (ed.). *Readings in Russian Poetics*. Ann Arbor, Mich., 1962.

MUKAŘOVSKÝ, J. *Estetická funkce, norma a hodnota*. Prague, 1936. [Reprinted in: *Studie z estetiky*. Prague, 1966. English translation in: *Michigan Slavic Contributions*, vol. III. Ann Arbor, Mich., 1970].

– *Kapitoly z české poetiky*, I–III. Prague, 1948.

POMORSKA, K. *Russian Formalist Theory and Its Poetic Ambiance*, The Hague – Paris, 1968.

VODIČKA, F. 'Literární historie. Její problémy a úkoly', *Čtení o jazyce a poesii*. Prague, 1942.

WELLEK, R., A. WARREN. *The Theory of Literature*. 2nd ed. New York, 1956.

3 THEORY OF NARRATIVE TEXT

BACHTIN, M.M. *Problemy tvorčestva Dostojevskogo*. Moscow, 1929. [2nd revised ed. under the title: *Problemy poetiki Dostojevskogo*. Moscow, 1963. French translation: *La poétique de Dostoievski*. Paris, 1970.]

BALLY, CH. 'Antiphrase et style indirect libre', *A Grammatical Miscellany Offered to Otto Jespersen*. Copenhagen – London, 1930.

– 'Figures de pensée et formes linguistiques', *Germanisch-Romanische Monatsschrift* (hereafter cited as *GRM*), VI (1914).

– 'Le style indirect libre en français moderne', *GRM*, IV (1912).

BARTHES, R. 'Introduction à l'analyse structurale des récits', *Communications*, VIII (1966).

– S/Z. Paris, 1970.

BOOTH, W.C. *The Rhetoric of Fiction*. Chicago – London, 1961.

BÜHLER, W. *Die 'erlebte Rede' im englischen Roman*. Schweizer anglistische Studien, vol. IV. n.p., n.d.

ČAPEK, K. 'Towards a Theory of Fairy-Tales', *In Praise of Newspapers and Other Essays on the Margin of Literature*. London, 1951.

DOLEŽEL, L. 'Nejtralizacija protivopostavlenij v jazykovo-stilističeskoj strukture epičeskoj prozy', *Problemy sovremennoj filologii*. Moscow. 1965.

– 'The Typology of the Narrator: Point of View in Fiction', *To Honor Roman Jakobson*, vol. I. The Hague, 1967.

ENGEL'GARDT, B.M. 'Ideologičeskij roman Dostojevskogo', *Dostojevskij. Statji i materialy*, vol. II. A. S. Dolinin (ed.). Leningrad, 1925.

FRIEDEMANN, K. *Die Rolle des Erzählers in der Epik*. Leipzig, 1910.

FRIEDMAN, N. 'Point of View in Fiction', *PMLA*, LXX (1955).

HALLER, J. 'Řeč přímá, nepřímá a polopřímá', *Naše řeč*, XIII (1929).

HOFFMEISTER, W. *Studien zur erlebten Rede bei Thomas Mann und Robert Musil*. The Hague, 1965.

KAYSER, W. 'Wer erzählt den Roman?', *Vortragsreise. Studien zur Literatur*. Bern, 1958.

KOFTUNOVA, I.I. 'Nesobstvenno-prjamaja reč' v sovremennom russkom literaturnom jazyke', *Russkij jazyk v škole*, no. 2 (1953).

KŘESÁLKOVÁ, J. 'Polopřímá řeč a nebezpečí, které v sobě skrývá pro překladatele', *Dialog*, I, no. 1 (1957).

KRISTEVA, J. *Le texte du roman*. The Hague – Paris, 1970.

LANDRY, A.G. *Represented Discourse in the Novels of François Mauriac*. Washington, DC, 1953.

LERCH, E. 'Ursprung und Bedeutung der sog. "erlebten Rede" (Rede als Tatsache)', *GRM*, XVI (1928).

LIPS, M. *Style indirect libre*. Paris, 1926.

LODGE, D. *Language of Fiction*. London – New York, 1966.

LORCK, E. *Die 'erlebte Rede'*. Heidelberg, 1921.

MERSEREAU, L. *Mikhail Lermontov*. Carbondale, Ill., 1962.

NEUBERT, A. *Die Stilformen der 'erlebten Rede' im neueren englischen Roman*. Halle-Saale, 1957.

POSPELOV, N.S. 'Nesobstvenno-prjamaja reč' i formy jeje vyraženija v chudožestvennoj proze Gončarova 30–40-ch godov', *Materialy i issledovanija po istorii russkogo literaturnogo jazyka*, vol. IV. Moscow, 1957.

POUILLON, J. *Temps et roman*. Paris, 1946.

PROPP, V. *Morfologija skazki*. Leningrad, 1928. [English translation: Bloomington, Indiana, 1958.]

PRŮŠEK, J. 'Quelques remarques sur la nouvelle littérature chinoise', *Mélanges de Sinologie offerts à M. Paul Demiéville*. Paris, 1966.

ROMBERG, B. *Studies in the Narrative Technique of the First-Person Novel*. Lund, 1962.

SCHOLES, R., R. KELLOGG, *The Nature of Narrative*. London – Oxford – New York, 1966.

ŠKLOVSKIJ, V. *O teorii prozy*. Moscow, 1925.

STANZEL, K.F. *Typische Formen des Romans*. Göttingen, 1964.

TITUNIK, I. 'The Problem of "Skaz" in Russian Literature', PhD. Dissertation, University of California, Berkeley, Calif., 1964.

TODOROV, T. 'Les catégories du récit littéraire', *Communications*, VIII (1966).

– *Grammaire du Décaméron*. The Hague – Paris, 1969.

VAN ROSSUM-GUYON, F. 'Point de vue ou perspective narrative', *Poétique*, IV (1970).

VINOGRADOV, V.V. *O chudožestvennoj proze*. Moscow – Leningrad, 1930.

– 'Stil' Pikovoj damy', *Puškin. Vremennik Puškinskoj komissii AN SSSR*, vol. II Moscow – Leningrad, 1936.

– 'O jazyke Tolstogo (50–60 gody)', *Literaturnoje nasledstvo*, XXXV–VI (1939).

4 STUDIES OF CZECH LITERATURE

BLAHYNKA, M. 'M. Kundera prozaik', *Plamen*, no. 1 (1967).

ČYŽEVŚKYJ, D. 'Das Labyrinth der Welt und das Paradies des Herzens des J.A. Comenius', *Wiener Slavistisches Jahrbuch*, V (1956).

DOLEŽEL, L. *O stylu moderní české prózy*. Prague, 1960.

DOLEŽEL, L., J. KUCHAŘ (eds.). *Knížka o jazyce a stylu soudobé české literatury*. Prague, 1961.

GRYGAR, M. 'Bedeutungsgehalt und Sujetafbau im *Pekař Jan Marhoul* von Vladislav Vančura', *Zeitschrift für Slawistik*, XIV (1969).

– *Rozbor moderní básnické epiky. Vančurův Pekař Jan Marhoul*. Rozpravy Československé akademie věd, Řada společenských věd, vol. I, Prague, 1970.

HARKINS, W. 'Imagery in Karel Čapek's *Hordubal*, *PMLA*, LXXV (1960).

– *Karel Čapek*. New York – London, 1962.

HEIDENREICH-DOLANSKÝ, J. 'K slovesné výstavbě mladých děl Komenského', *Český časopis filologický*, II (1943–4).

JAKOBSON, R. 'Dvě staročeské skladby o smrti', Foreword to *Spor duše s tělem*. Prague, 1927.

JANÁČKOVÁ, J. *Český román na sklonku 19. století*. Prague, 1967.

– 'Jiráskovo vypravěčství, jeho charakter a funkce', *Česká literatura*, XV (1967).

JEDLIČKA, A. 'Spisovný jazyk a nářečí v Mrštíkově Roku na vsi', *Pocta Fr. Trávníčkovi a Fr. Wollmanovi*. Brno, 1948.

MUKAROVSKÝ, J. 'Protichůdci', *Slovo a slovesnost*, II (1936).

NEEDHAM, J. (ed.). *The Teacher of Nations*. Cambridge, 1942.

POHORSKÝ, M. 'Komika Kunderova Žertu', *Česká literatura*, XVII (1969).

SADLER, J.E. *J.A. Comenius and the Concept of Universal Education.* London, 1966.

SCHAMSCHULA, W. 'Der sakrale Stil und seine Funktion im Werk Karel Čapeks', *Slawistische Studien zum V. Internationalen Slawistenkongress in Sofia 1963.* M. Braun, E. Koschmieder, I. Mahnken (eds.). Göttingen, 1963.

ŠKARKA, A. *Afterword to Labyrint světa a ráj srdce.* Prague, 1958.

SPINKA, M. *John A. Comenius: That Incomparable Moravian.* Chicago, Ill., 1943.

VODIČKA, F. *Počátky krásné prózy novočeské.* Prague, 1948.

WELLEK, R. *Essays on Czech Literature.* The Hague, 1963.

Index

CENTRE FOR RUSSIAN AND EAST EUROPEAN STUDIES
UNIVERSITY OF TORONTO

Feeding the Russian Fur Trade. James R. Gibson. University of Wisconsin Press, Madison, 1969

The Czech Renascence of the Nineteenth Century: essays in honour of Otakar Odložilik. Edited by Peter Brock and H. Gordon Skilling. University of Toronto Press, 1970

The Soviet Wood-Processing Industry: a linear programming analysis of the role of transportation costs in location and flow patterns. Brenton M. Barr. University of Toronto Press, 1970

Interest Groups in Soviet Politics. Edited by H. Gordon Skilling and Franklyn Griffiths. Princeton University Press, 1971

Between Gogol and Ševčenko. George S. N. Luckyj. Harvard Series in Ukrainian Studies, Wilhelm Fink Verlag, Munich, 1971

The Collective Farm in Soviet Agriculture. Robert C. Stuart. D.C. Heath and Company, Lexington, Mass., 1972

Guide to the Decisions of the Communist Party of the Soviet Union 1917–1967. Robert H. McNeal. University of Toronto Press, 1973

Leon Trotsky and the Politics of Economic Isolation. Richard B. Day. Cambridge University Press, 1973

Narrative Modes in Czech Literature. Lubomír Doležel. University of Toronto Press, 1973

Soviet Urban Politics. Michael B. Frolic. The MIT Press, forthcoming